子鼠，丑牛，寅虎，卯兔，辰龙，巳蛇，午马，未羊，申猴、酉鸡、戌狗、亥猪。

十二生肖
CHINESE ZODIAC

本教材为 2016 年度教育部哲学社会科学研究重大课题攻关项目
"中国书法文化国际传播的理论与实践研究"（16JZD031）阶段性成果
并获得 2020 年度上海市"中华文化走出去"专项扶持资金支持

"风调雨顺"系列教材

12 Chinese Zodiacs

"Season with Timely Breeze and Rain for Crop Raising" Coursebook Series

主编：周斌　周佳楠
Editor-in-chief: ZHOU Bin, ZHOU Jianan

副主编：Roy Ye　尹冬民
Associate Editor: Roy Ye, YIN Dongmin

插图：孙凌雁
Illustrator: SUN Lingyan

书法：盛兰军
Calligraphy: SHENG Lanjun

翻译：吴顺俪
Translators: WU Shunli

手工制作：单亚琴
Handcrafty: SHAN Yaqin

书籍设计：周佳楠
Graphic Designer: ZHOU Jianan

华东师范大学出版社

Dear kids, do you know these two characters?
They are good friends. Panda Nini lives in China, while Chicken Jerry lives in the USA. Every year they write to each other to send their best regards. One year during Chinese New Year, Nini invited Jerry to come to China as a guest. Nini introduced Jerry to the tradition of Chinese New Year and told him that this year people were welcoming the Year of the Rat, one of the 12 zodiac signs in the Chinese legend. Jerry was very curious about the 12 Chinese zodiac signs and wanted Nini to tell him more about these animals. Now, dear kids, let's join Nini to get to know these lovely animals!

　　小朋友们，你们认识它们俩吗？

　　它们俩呀是一对好朋友。熊猫妮妮生活在中国，小鸡杰瑞住在美国。它们每年都会写信问候彼此。有一年春节，妮妮邀请杰瑞来中国做客，妮妮向杰瑞介绍了春节的习俗，并告诉它今年人们正在迎接十二生肖中的鼠年的到来。杰瑞对十二生肖十分好奇，一定要妮妮给它讲讲这些生肖的故事。小朋友们，让我们跟着妮妮一起来了解一下这些可爱的生肖吧。

> Nini, what are the 12 Chinese zodiacs?

> Jerry, the Chinese zodiacs are also called Shuxiang in Chinese. The 12 Chinese zodiacs are matched by the 12 Earthly Branches (Dizhi), with 12 animals that represent the birth year of each human being. The 12 animals are Rat, Ox, Tiger, Rabbit, Dragon, Snake, Horse, Goat, Monkey, Rooster, Dog and Pig. The 12 Earthly Branches (Dizhi) are the traditional Chinese way of recording time, including Zi, Chou, Yin, Mao, Chen, Si, Wu, Wei, Shen, You, Xu, Hai. They represent the different time periods in a day. Chinese ancestors used these 12 animals to match the various Earthly Branches (Dizhi), which led to the saying of Zi Rat, Chou Ox, Yin Tiger, Mao Rabbit, Chen Dragon, Si Snake, Wu Horse, Wei Goat, Shen Monkey, You Rooster, Xu Dog and Hai Pig.

Note: Earthly Branches (Dizhi) match with Heavenly Stems (Tiangan) and they will be combined as Ganzhi. 10 Heavenly Stems (Tiangan) and 12 Earthly Branches (Dizhi) in total have 60 combinations, which are used to show the order of the year, month and date repeatedly in this cycle. Years in modern Chinese lunar calendar are still employing this Ganzhi way of recording.

妮妮，什么是十二生肖呢？

杰瑞，生肖又叫属相，十二生肖是与十二地支相配用来代表人们出生年份的十二种动物，包括鼠、牛、虎、兔、龙、蛇、马、羊、猴、鸡、狗、猪。而十二地支是中国传统的纪时方法，包括子、丑、寅、卯、辰、巳、午、未、申、酉、戌、亥，代表了一天中不同的时间段。古人以这十二种动物来匹配各个地支，因而产生了子鼠、丑牛、寅虎、卯兔、辰龙、巳蛇、午马、未羊、申猴、酉鸡、戌狗、亥猪的说法。

注：地支与天干相配，合称干支。十天干和十二地支共配成六十组，用来表示年、月、日的次序，周而复始，循环往复。现代中国农历的年份仍用干支纪年法。

 The legend begins

It is said that, a long, long time ago, the Jade Emperor found out that it was too hard for people to remember years while remembering the names of animals seemed to be easier. So he told Servant Earth to announce the news of choosing 12 animals which would be assigned to a repeating twelve-year cycle.

The animals were quite excited to hear the news and all of them wanted to participate in the race. What happened in the Big Race? Let's go and have a look!

Participants would have a Big Race of crossing the river and the first 12 animals who arrived at the finishing line would be announced as the 12 Chinese zodiacs.

故事开始了

相传古时候玉皇大帝发现人们记年份太难了,而记动物的名字就容易多了,于是通知土地公公,让他去发布选拔十二生肖的消息。

动物们听到消息都很兴奋,都想参加比赛。究竟比赛过程是怎样的呢?让我们一起来看一下吧!

参加选拔的动物们比赛渡河,按照到达终点的顺序,前十二名即为十二生肖。

目录

十二生肖

NO.1 鼠 (Shu)
Rat
鼠的故事 / 3
跟着妮妮学一学 / 4
跟着杰瑞写一写 / 5
玩一玩、画一画 / 6
想一想、说一说 / 7
属鼠的书法家 / 8

NO.2 牛 (Niu)
Ox
牛的故事 / 11
跟着妮妮学一学 / 12
跟着杰瑞写一写 / 13
玩一玩、画一画 / 14
想一想、说一说 / 15
属牛的书法家 / 16

NO.3 虎 (Hu)
Tiger
虎的故事 / 19
跟着妮妮学一学 / 20
跟着杰瑞写一写 / 21
玩一玩、画一画 / 22
想一想、说一说 / 23
属虎的书法家 / 24

NO.4 兔 (Tu)
Rabbit
兔的故事 / 27
跟着妮妮学一学 / 28
跟着杰瑞写一写 / 29
玩一玩、画一画 / 30
想一想、说一说 / 31
属兔的书法家 / 32

NO.5 龙 (Long)
Dragon
龙的故事 / 35
跟着妮妮学一学 / 36
跟着杰瑞写一写 / 37
玩一玩、画一画 / 38
想一想、说一说 / 39
属龙的书法家 / 40

NO.6 蛇 (She)
Snake
蛇的故事 / 43
跟着妮妮学一学 / 44
跟着杰瑞写一写 / 45
玩一玩、画一画 / 46
想一想、说一说 / 47
属蛇的书法家 / 48

目 录

十二生肖

NO.7 马 (Ma) Horse
马的故事 / 51
跟着妮妮学一学 / 52
跟着杰瑞写一写 / 53
玩一玩、画一画 / 54
想一想、说一说 / 55
属马的书法家 / 56

NO.8 羊 (Yang) Goat
羊的故事 / 59
跟着妮妮学一学 / 60
跟着杰瑞写一写 / 61
玩一玩、画一画 / 62
想一想、说一说 / 63
属羊的书法家 / 64

NO.9 猴 (Hou) Monkey
猴的故事 / 67
跟着妮妮学一学 / 68
跟着杰瑞写一写 / 69
玩一玩、画一画 / 70
想一想、说一说 / 71
属猴的书法家 / 72

NO.10 鸡 (Ji) Rooster
鸡的故事 / 75
跟着妮妮学一学 / 76
跟着杰瑞写一写 / 77
玩一玩、画一画 / 78
想一想、说一说 / 79
属鸡的书法家 / 80

NO.11 狗 (Gou) Dog
狗的故事 / 83
跟着妮妮学一学 / 84
跟着杰瑞写一写 / 85
玩一玩、画一画 / 86
想一想、说一说 / 87
属狗的书法家 / 88

NO.12 猪 (Zhu) Pig
猪的故事 / 91
跟着妮妮学一学 / 92
跟着杰瑞写一写 / 93
玩一玩、画一画 / 94
想一想、说一说 / 95
属猪的书法家 / 97

后记 / 98

Contents

12 Chinese zodiacs

No.1 鼠 (Shu) Rat
The story of Rat / 2
Learning calligraphy with Nini / 4
Practicing calligraphy with Jerry / 5
Playing and painting / 6
Thinking and talking / 7
A calligrapher born in the Year of the Rat / 8

No.2 牛 (Niu) Ox
The story of Ox / 10
Learning calligraphy with Nini / 12
Practicing calligraphy with Jerry / 13
Playing and painting / 14
Thinking and talking / 15
A calligrapher born in the Year of the Ox / 16

No.3 虎 (Hu) Tiger
The story of Tiger / 18
Learning calligraphy with Nini / 20
Practicing calligraphy with Jerry / 21
Playing and painting / 22
Thinking and talking / 23
A calligrapher born in the Year of the Tiger / 24

No.4 兔 (Tu) Rabbit
The story of Rabbit / 26
Learning calligraphy with Nini / 28
Practicing calligraphy with Jerry / 29
Playing and painting / 30
Thinking and talking / 31
A calligrapher born in the Year of the Rabbit / 32

No.5 龙 (Long) Dragon
The story of Dragon / 34
Learning calligraphy with Nini / 36
Practicing calligraphy with Jerry / 37
Playing and painting / 38
Thinking and talking / 39
A calligrapher born in the Year of the Dragon / 40

No.6 蛇 (She) Snake
The story of Snake / 42
Learning calligraphy with Nini / 44
Practicing calligraphy with Jerry / 45
Playing and painting / 46
Thinking and talking / 47
A calligrapher born in the Year of the Snake / 48

Contents

12 Chinese zodiacs

NO.7 马 (Ma) Horse

The story of Horse / 50

Learning calligraphy with Nini / 52

Practicing calligraphy with Jerry / 53

Playing and painting / 54

Thinking and talking / 55

A calligrapher born in the Year of the Horse / 56

NO.8 羊 (Yang) Goat

The story of Goat / 58

Learning calligraphy with Nini / 60

Practicing calligraphy with Jerry / 61

Playing and painting / 62

Thinking and talking / 63

A calligrapher born in the Year of the Goat / 64

NO.9 猴 (Hou) Monkey

The story of Monkey / 66

Learning calligraphy with Nini / 68

Practicing calligraphy with Jerry / 69

Playing and painting / 70

Thinking and talking / 71

A calligrapher born in the Year of the Monkey / 72

NO.10 鸡 (Ji) Rooster

The story of Rooster / 74

Learning calligraphy with Nini / 76

Practicing calligraphy with Jerry / 77

Playing and painting / 78

Thinking and talking / 79

A calligrapher born in the Year of the Rooster / 80

NO.11 狗 (Gou) Dog

The story of Dog / 82

Learning calligraphy with Nini / 84

Practicing calligraphy with Jerry / 85

Playing and painting / 86

Thinking and talking / 87

A calligrapher born in the Year of the Dog / 88

NO.12 猪 (Zhu) Pig

The story of Pig / 90

Learning calligraphy with Nini / 92

Practicing calligraphy with Jerry / 93

Playing and painting / 94

Thinking and talking / 95

A calligrapher born in the Year of the Pig / 96

Postscript / 100

Shu
鼠 Rat

The story of Rat

A long, long time ago, Cat and Rat were good friends. They decided to register for the Big Race together when they heard the news of choosing the 12 Chinese zodiacs. Cat was worried that she would be late, so she told Rat to wake her up when it was time for the registration. However, Rat was only thinking about registering for himself and completely forgot Cat's words. Therefore, Cat missed the chance of becoming one of the 12 zodiacs and had been the enemy of Rat ever since.

During the Big Race, seeing that Ox was quite strong and strode with big steps, Rat was afraid that he might not be able to catch up with Ox, so he made up a plan and said to Ox. "Hi, Brother, shall I lie prone on your back and sing songs for you near your ear?" Ox thought it would be great to listen to songs while running in the race, so he agreed without any hesitation. Thus, Rat got to ride on Ox's back and sang songs along the way. While they approached the finish line, Rat quickly jumped off Ox's back and, unexpectedly, became the first to arrive. That was how Rat became the first of the 12 Chinese zodiacs.

The characteristics of people who were born in the Year of the Rat: they have a positive attitude; they are diligent and hardworking, smart and crafty and they have a strong ability in adapting to the environment.

鼠的故事

那时候,猫和老鼠是好朋友。听到选拔十二生肖的消息,它们决定去报名。猫担心自己迟到,就让老鼠到时候叫醒它。可老鼠只想着给自己报名,把猫的嘱托给忘了。就这样,猫错过了入选十二生肖的机会,它也因此跟老鼠结了仇。

渡河比赛中,老鼠看到牛块头大,迈的步子也大,自己根本赶不上,于是心生一计,对牛说:"牛哥哥,我趴在你耳边为你唱歌好吗?"牛心想能边跑边听歌,那多好啊,于是就爽快地答应了。就这样,老鼠骑在牛背上,唱了一路的歌。没想到快到终点时,老鼠吱溜一声,纵身一跃跳到了牛的前面,抢得了第一名,就这样排在了十二生肖的首位。

生肖为鼠的人性格特点:做事积极,勤奋努力;头脑机智,手脚灵巧;对环境的适应能力强。

跟着妮妮学一学
Learning calligraphy with Nini

篆书 (zhuan shu) | Seal script

"子"字从篆书字形上看像婴儿舞动双臂的样子。本义表示婴儿。又指地支的第一位。

The character of "子 (zi)" in seal script looks like a baby waving both arms. Its original meaning is a baby. It is also used to indicate the first place of Earthly Branches (Dizhi).

篆书"鼠"字由上下两部分组成,它的上半部分像张口露出牙齿的鼠的头部,下半部分像老鼠的足和尾。因老鼠的牙齿十分厉害,故字形中强调老鼠的利齿。

The character of "鼠 (shu)" in seal script consists of two parts. The upper part looks like the head of a rat that opens its mouth and shows its teeth. The lower part looks like the feet and tail of the rat. As a rat's teeth are considered very fierce, the rat's teeth are especially emphasized in the character.

扫描右侧二维码,让我们一起来欣赏"鼠"字的动画故事吧!

Let's scan the QR code on the right to enjoy the animation story of the Character "鼠".

在学写"子鼠"之前，我们先来学习书法中一些常见的基本笔画。之后大家可以举一反三进行练习。

Before we start writing "子鼠", let's learn some fundamental strokes in Chinese calligraphy first. Then you will be able to apply them to your later practice.

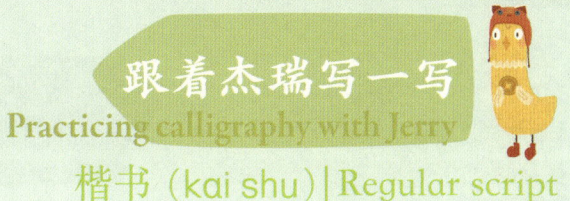

楷书 (kai shu) | Regular script

フ 了 子

′ ⺊ ⺊ 臼 臼 臼 臼 臼 臼 鼠 鼠 鼠

扫描右侧二维码，一起来学习它们的基本写法吧！

Let's scan the QR code on the right to watch the videos to learn how to write the characters.

玩一玩、画一画
Playing and painting

跟着妮妮和杰瑞
做送给朋友的
礼物

Follow Nini and Jerry to make gifts for your friends.

杰瑞的画
Jerry's painting

妮妮的手工
Nini's handcraft

想一想、说一说
Thinking and talking

与妮妮和杰瑞一起想一想
Think with Nini and Jerry:
你认识的哪些人是鼠年出生的？他们是什么星座？
Who do you know was born in the Year of the Rat? What are their astrological signs?

鼠年的年份
The Year of the Rat
1900年、1912年、1924年、1936年、1948年、1960年、1972年、1984年、1996年、2008年。

鼠年出生的名人
Celebrities born in the Year of the Rat:
杜甫、金庸、莎士比亚、乔治·华盛顿、伽利略。
Du Fu (a poet of Tang Dynasty), Jin Yong (an author of some kunfu novels), William Shakespeare, George Washington, Galileo Galilei.

与妮妮和杰瑞一起比赛
Compete with Nini and Jerry:
说出与"鼠"有关的词语或成语。
Say the words or proverbs related with the word "Shu (Rat)".

A calligrapher born in the Year of the Rat

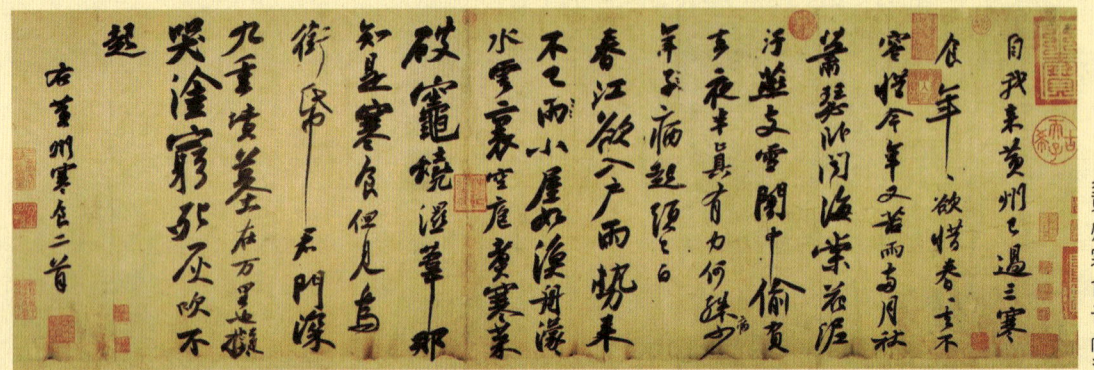

《黄州寒食诗帖》

苏轼（1037—1101），北宋著名文学家、书法家、画家，"宋四家"之一。书法用笔多取侧势、结体扁平稍肥。书风早年姿媚、中年圆劲、晚年沉着。《黄州寒食诗帖》是其中年代表作，笔墨随着诗句语境的变化而跌宕起伏，一气呵成，达到"心手双畅"的完美境界。

Su Shi (1037—1101), was a famous literator, calligrapher and painter of Northern Song Dynasty, as one of the "Four Masters of Song Dynasty". His brush took more side potential with a flat and fat structure. His calligraphy style was exquisite at early age, strong in middle age and placid in later life. *Poems Written at Huang-chou on the Cold Food Festival Tie* was his representative work of his middle age. The writing strokes and strength fluctuated with the context of the poem, and the whole post was completed within one creation, indicating the beauty of "the harmony of hands and mind".

Niu
牛 Ox

The story of Ox

Ox was running all the way in the race. After climbing onto the other bank of the river, he was very happy to rush to the end. Unexpectedly, Rat jumped down from Ox's back and reached the finish line ahead of Ox. Ox worked so hard but Rat finally took advantage of his work. Ox was very angry, for he only arrived in the second place. He started to keep his big eyes open all the time and had been watchful ever since.

The characteristics of people who were born in the Year of the Ox: they are diligent and hardworking; they have a strong initiative; they are honest and tolerant, practical, responsible, and endurable.

牛的故事

牛在比赛中一路狂奔,爬上河对岸后,正准备高高兴兴地冲向终点,却没想到老鼠从它的背上跳了下来,抢先一步抵达终点。牛辛苦了半天却被老鼠占了便宜,只得了第二名,它非常生气。从此呀牛就一直瞪着大眼睛。

生肖为牛的人性格特点：勤奋努力,有强烈的进取心;忠厚老实,务实,责任心强,有耐力。

跟着妮妮学一学
Learning calligraphy with Nini

篆书（zhuan shu）| Seal script

"丑"字从篆书字形上看像手指勾曲用力揪东西的形状，本义是纽、连接。现在多用来形容相貌难看。又指地支的第二位。

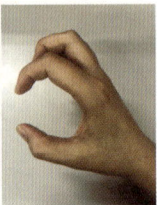

The character of "丑 (chou)" in seal script looks like the shape that fingers are crooking and pulling something hard. Its original meaning is twisting and connecting. Today it is usually used to describe ugliness in appearance. It is also used to indicate the second place of Earthly Branches (Dizhi).

"牛"字从篆书字形上看，上半部分像向两侧伸出的一对弧形的牛角，下半部分像简化了的牛头，突出了牛耳的形状。本义指家畜牛。

The character of "牛 (niu)" in seal script has two parts. The upper part looks like a pair of curved bull horns stretching out to two sides while the lower part looks like a simplified bull head highlighting the shape of the Ox's ears. Its original meaning is cattle.

扫描右侧二维码，让我们一起来欣赏"牛"字的动画故事吧！
Let's scan the QR code on the right to enjoy the animation story of the Character "牛".

扫描右侧二维码，一起来学习它们的基本写法吧！
Let's scan the QR code on the right to watch the videos to learn how to write the characters.

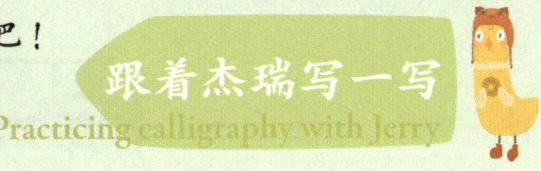

楷书（kai shu）| Regular script

丁 刀 丑 丑

丿 二 牛

玩一玩、画一画
Playing and painting

跟着妮妮和杰瑞
做送给朋友的
礼物

Follow Nini and Jerry to
make gifts for your friends.

杰瑞的画
Jerry's painting

妮妮的手工
Nini's handcraft

想一想、说一说
Thinking and talking

与妮妮和杰瑞一起想一想
Think with Nini and Jerry:
你认识的哪些人是牛年出生的？他们是什么星座？
Who do you know was born in the Year of the Ox? What are their astrological signs?

牛年的年份
The Year of the Ox
1901年、1913年、1925年、1937年、1949年、1961年、1973年、1985年、1997年、2009年。

牛年出生的名人
Celebrities born in the Year of the Ox:
刘备、陶渊明、李白、拿破仑、安徒生。
Liu Bei (the first emperor of the state of Shu in the Three Kingdoms Period), Tao Yuanming (a poet from Jin Dynasty), Li Bai (a poet from Tang Dynasty), Napoléon Bonaparte, Hans Christian Andersen.

与妮妮和杰瑞一起比赛
Compete with Nini and Jerry:
说出与"牛"有关的词语或成语。
Say the words or proverbs related with the word "Niu (Ox)".

A calligrapher born in the Year of the Ox

《九成宫醴泉铭》

欧阳询（557—641），初唐四大家之一。书法风格严谨工整、平正峭劲。《九成宫醴泉铭》是欧体楷书的登峰造极之作，字形稍长，布白均匀，中宫紧密，主笔突出，显得气势奔放，气韵生动。字体结构大都向右扩展，但重心稳固，无倾侧之感，寓险于正。

Ouyang Xun (557—641), was one of the four masters of the early Tang Dynasty. His calligraphy style is precise, neat and straight. *Inscription on Sweet-Water Spring at Jiucheng Palace* is one of the masterpieces of Ouyang Xun's style in regular script. The font is slightly longer and evenly distributed with a compact middle section and a prominent main stroke, indicating a vigorous and unrestrained spirit. The structure of the characters is mostly extended to the right side without causing any sense of imbalance or tilt with a perfect imbalance balanced. But the center of gravity is stable and there is no sense of tilting, with risks in positive.

Hu
虎 Tiger

The story of Tiger

Tiger also participated in the 12 Chinese zodiacs selection competition. When he swam to the other side of the river bank with water all over him, he shouted quite confidently, "I shall be the first!" The Jade Emperor said, "No, you are the third." As a matter of fact, Tiger ended up being put behind Rat and Ox.

The characteristics of people who were born in the Year of the Tiger: they are full of vigor and vitality, so they are ambitious; they dare to think and act, so they dare to blaze new trails; they are passionate and generous, indomitable and confident; they also have a sense of justice and are willing to help others.

虎的故事

老虎也参加了十二生肖选拔比赛,当它湿淋淋地游到河对岸时,它很自信地吼着:"我是第一名吧!"玉皇大帝说:"不!你是第三名。"没办法,最后老虎只能排在了鼠和牛的后面。

生肖为虎的人性格特点　朝气蓬勃,有雄心壮志;敢想敢干,勇于开拓;热情大方,顽强自信;有正义感,乐于助人。

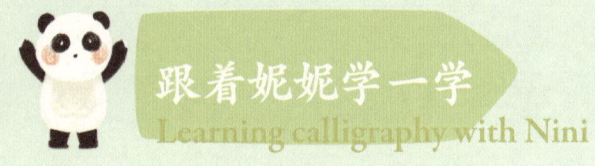

跟着妮妮学一学
Learning calligraphy with Nini
篆书 (zhuan shu) | Seal script

"寅"字从篆书字形上看像在"矢"的字形上加一圈指事符号，表示箭矢穿透匣子。本义指从匣子中取出箭矢。又指地支的第三位。

The character of "寅 (yin)" in seal script looks like adding some indicative symbols around the character of "矢 (shi)", which means that an arrow goes through a box. Its original meaning is to get the arrow out of a box. It is also used to indicate the third place of Earthly Branches (Dizhi).

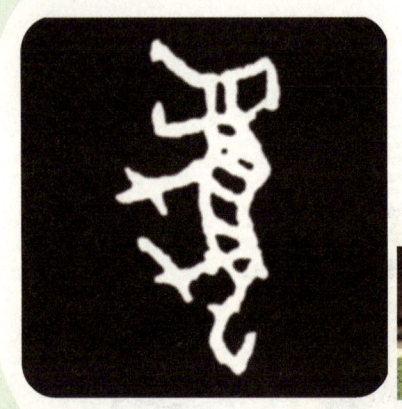

"虎"字从篆书字形上看像大嘴巨身，身带花纹，外形威猛的老虎的样子，本义指会袭击人类的山中兽王。

The character of "虎(hu)" in seal script looks like the figure of a fierce tiger with a big mouth and giant body with decorative stripe. Its original meaning is the king in the forest that may attack people.

扫描右侧二维码，让我们一起来欣赏"虎"字的动画故事吧！

Let's scan the QR code on the right to enjoy the animation story of the Character "虎".

扫描右侧二维码，一起来学习它们的基本写法吧！

Let's scan the QR code on the right to watch the videos to learn how to write the characters.

跟着杰瑞写一写
Practicing calligraphy with Jerry

楷书（kai shu）| Regular script

玩一玩、画一画
Playing and painting

跟着妮妮和杰瑞做送给朋友的 **礼物**

Follow Nini and Jerry to make gifts for your friends.

杰瑞的画
Jerry's painting

黄虎

妮妮的手工
Nini's handcraft

想一想、说一说
Thinking and talking

与妮妮和杰瑞一起想一想
Think with Nini and Jerry:
你认识的哪些人
是虎年出生的？
他们是什么星座？
Who do you know was born in the Year of the Tiger? What are their astrological signs?

虎年的年份
The Year of the Tiger
1902年、1914年、
1926年、1938年、
1950年、1962年、
1974年、1986年、
1998年、2010年。

虎年出生的名人
Celebrities born in the Year of the Tiger:
秦始皇、李时珍、
孙中山、贝多芬、
马可·波罗。
First Emperor of Qin (China's first emperor who built the Great Wall), Li Shizhen (a doctor who studied herbs), Sun Yat-sen (the founder of the Republic of China), Ludwig van Beethoven, Marco Polo.

与妮妮和杰瑞一起比赛
Compete with Nini and Jerry:
说出与"虎"
有关的词语或
成语。
Say the words or proverbs related with the word "Hu (Tiger)".

A calligrapher born in the Year of the Tiger

《洛神赋》

赵孟頫（1254—1322），南宋末至元初著名书法家、画家、诗人。书风秀逸，结体严整、笔法圆熟，创"赵体"书。《洛神赋》结构端正匀称、字姿优美潇洒、运笔圆润灵秀、布局密中有疏，端美中具俯仰起伏的气势，显示出他博取众长而自成一体的艺术特色。

Zhao Mengfu (1254—1322), was a famous calligrapher, painter and poet of the late Southern Song Dynasty and early Yuan Dynasty. His calligraphy style is elegant in a neat structure and his brushwork presents dexterity, forming a unique "Zhao Style". *Ode to the Goddess of the Luo River* has regular and symmetrical structures, with graceful and unrestrained composition, delicate and refined handling, and changes in density. The flowing brushwork indicates that he was inspired from other established artists' works and his continuous calligraphy revolution. He had adopted useful skills from others and formed his independent artistic feature.

Tu 兔 Rabbit

The story of Rabbit

Rabbit was the neighbor of Ox. They had made a promise to each other that they would get up together when the rooster crowed the first time on the morning of the 12 Chinese zodiacs selection competition day so that they could participate the Big Race. When the rooster crowed the first time, Ox got up just to find out that Rabbit had already left. Rabbit ran for a while and looked back, finding nobody behind. Rabbit thought to himself: I got up earliest this morning and ran fastest. I would still be the first to cross the river even after having a nap. Therefore, Rabbit lay down on the grassland and sank into a deep sleep. While Rabbit was still in his sound sleep, Ox had crossed the finish line. Rabbit was awoken by the sound of several rapid footsteps. He opened his eyes and realized that Tiger had just run past him like a blast of wind. Rabbit got anxious and hurriedly began racing again. Unfortunately, he was still one step behind and lost to Tiger, becoming the fourth animal to cross the finish line.

The characteristics of people who were born in the Year of the Rabbit: they are gentle, kind, optimistic, and they have subtle and refined sensibilities; they are quick-witted; they are tolerant, modest and non-controversial.

兔的故事

兔子和牛是邻居，它们相互约定，生肖选拔那天，鸡叫头遍就一起起床参加渡河比赛，争取入选十二生肖。到了生肖选拔的日子，鸡叫头遍，牛起床时，发现兔子早就自己先跑了。兔子跑了好一阵子，回头一看，不见任何动物的影子。兔子心想，我今天起得最早，跑得又最快，就是睡上一觉起来再渡河也来得及。于是，它在草地上呼呼大睡起来。当兔子还在酣睡的时候，牛已经抵达了终点。突然一阵急促的脚步声惊醒了兔子，它睁眼一看，原来是老虎一阵风般地从它身边跑了过去。这下兔子急了，赶紧起身追赶，可惜还是慢了一步，最终落在了老虎的后面，排在第四名。

生肖为兔的人性格特点：温柔、善良、乐观，感情细腻；精明灵活；忍耐谦让，不好争执。

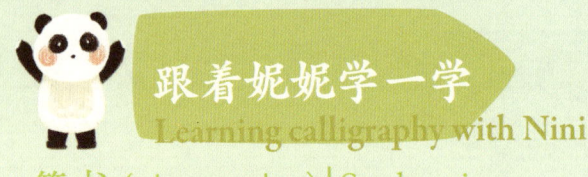

跟着妮妮学一学
Learning calligraphy with Nini
篆书 (zhuan shu) | Seal script

"卯"字是指事字，从篆书字形上看像开门的样子。本义指万物破土生长。又指地支的第四位。

The character of "卯 (mao)" in seal script is a self-explanatory character, the shape of which looks like a door that is open. Its original meaning is that everything breaks through the soil. It is also used to indicate the fourth place of Earthly Branches (Dizhi).

"兔"字从篆书字形上看像一只头大耳长、尾巴短小的小兔子的侧视图。

The character of "兔(tu)" in seal script looks like the profile of a rabbit, which has a big head, long ears, and a short unbending tail.

扫描右侧二维码，让我们一起来欣赏"兔"字的动画故事吧！

Let's scan the QR code on the right to enjoy the animation story of the Character "兔".

扫描右侧二维码，一起来学习它们的基本写法吧！

Let's scan the QR code on the right to watch the videos to learn how to write the characters.

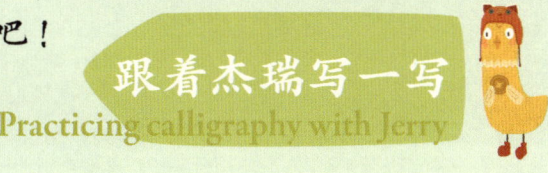

跟着杰瑞写一写
Practicing calligraphy with Jerry

楷书（kai shu）| Regular script

丶 𠃋 𠂎 𠨍 卯

丿 𠂉 𠂆 𠂈 𠂊 𠂋 兔 兔

玩一玩、画一画
Playing and painting

跟着妮妮和杰瑞
做送给朋友的
礼物

Follow Nini and Jerry to make gifts for your friends.

杰瑞的画
Jerry's painting

妮妮的手工
Nini's handcraft

想一想、说一说
Thinking and talking

与妮妮和杰瑞一起想一想
Think with Nini and Jerry:
你认识的哪些人是兔年出生的？他们是什么星座？
Who do you know was born in the Year of the Rabbit? What are their astrological signs?

兔年的年份
The Year of the Rabbit
1903年、1915年、1927年、1939年、1951年、1963年、1975年、1987年、1999年、2011年。

兔年出生的名人
Celebrities born in the Year of the Rabbit:
曹丕、米芾、胡适、阿尔伯特·爱因斯坦、迈克尔·乔丹。
Cao Pi (the first emperor of the state of Wei in the Three Kingdoms Period), Mi Fu (a calligrapher), Hu Shi (a Chinese philosopher and diplomat), Albert Einstein, Michael Jordan.

与妮妮和杰瑞一起比赛
Compete with Nini and Jerry:
说出与"兔"有关的词语或成语。
Say the words or proverbs related with the word "Tu (Rabbit)".

31

A calligrapher born in the Year of the Rabbit

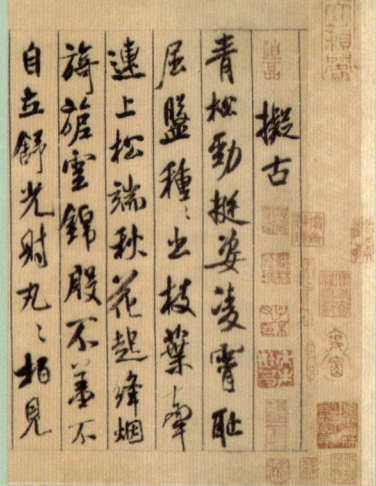
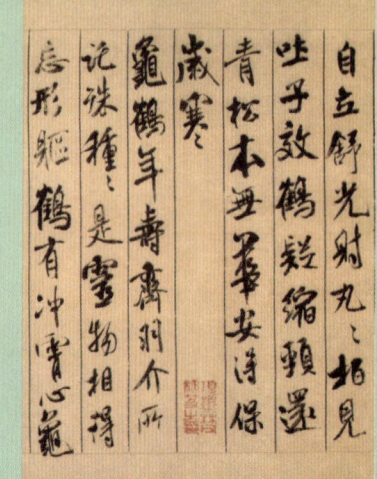

《蜀素帖》

米芾（1051—1107），北宋书法家、画家、书画理论家，"宋四家"之一。书法用笔八面出锋，于变化中显沉着笔力，正侧藏露，动荡摇曳，体态万千，充分体现了其"刷"字之风。《蜀素帖》笔法跳荡精致、结体变化多端、笔势沉着痛快，被誉为"中华第一美帖"。

Mi Fu (1051—1107), was a calligrapher, painter and theorist of the Northern Song Dynasty, as one of the "Four Masters of Song Dynasty". His brush strokes come out from eight sides, showing his composure in changes. The brushwork is full of fluctuations and modeling, which forms Mi's "brush" style. *Poems Written on Sichuan Silk is* known as "the most beautiful script in China" because of its swift-changing and delicate brushwork, diverse structures, steady and elegant writing style.

Long
龙 Dragon

The story of Dragon

While the competition was intense, suddenly, a gust of wind rolled up from the sky. Dragon descended from the sky to participate in the race. Just before he crossed the finish line, Rabbit beat him to it. The Jade Emperor asked Dragon, "As you were flying all the way, how come you came so late?" It turned out that Dragon was hosting the raining ceremony in the South China Sea and when he came here he was already late for the competition. Thus, Dragon only got the fifth place in the competition.

The characteristics of people who were born in the Year of the Dragon: they keep going forward courageously and they have a strong initiative; they are assertive and focused and decisive; they are generous, confident and talented.

龙的故事

正当比赛在紧张地进行时，突然间，天空卷起一阵狂风，龙从天而降，眼看就要抵达终点，却被兔子抢先了一步。玉皇大帝问："你是飞来的，怎么这么晚才到呢？"原来，龙去南海主持下雨典礼了，赶回来时已经来不及了，只获得了比赛的第五名。

生肖为龙的人性格特点　勇往直前，有强烈的进取心；专心致志，果敢坚定；慷慨，自信，有才能。

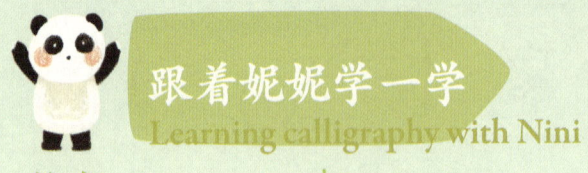

跟着妮妮学一学
Learning calligraphy with Nini
篆书 (zhuan shu) | Seal script

篆书"辰"字上部分的短横表示地表，整个字描绘的是蛰虫在惊蛰时苏醒后蠢蠢欲动的样子。引申指震动。后意为日、月、星的总称，又为时间、日子。又指地支的第五位。

The short horizontal stroke on top of the character of "辰(chen)" in seal script indicates the ground surface. The whole character is describing the appearance of the restless insects after they get woken up around the period of the Waking of Insects. It is also extended to mean vibration. Later, it becomes the general term of the sun, the moon and the stars and also means the time and the date. It is also used to indicate the fifth place of Earthly Branches(Dizhi).

"龙"字从篆书字形上看描绘的是一种动物形象——有头有角，口大张，并露出锋利的牙齿，有着弯弯曲曲的身子。本义指我国古代传说中的一种神异动物。封建时代龙被作为帝王的象征。

The character of "龙(long)" in seal script is describing the image of an animal which has a head, horns, a wide-open mouth, sharp teeth and bending body. Its original meaning is a miraculous animal in the ancient legend in our county. In feudal times, the dragon was considered to be the symbol of the emperor.

扫描右侧二维码，让我们一起来欣赏"龙"字的动画故事吧！
Let's scan the QR code on the right to enjoy the animation story of the Character "龙".

扫描右侧二维码，一起来学习它们的基本写法吧！

Let's scan the QR code on the right to watch the videos to learn how to write the characters.

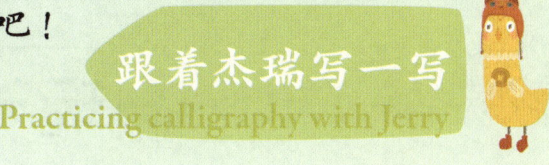

跟着杰瑞写一写

Practicing calligraphy with Jerry

楷书（kai shu）| Regular script

一 厂 厂 厂 戸 辰 辰 辰

丶 亠 六 立 产 音 音 音 音 音 音 龍 龍 龍 龍

玩一玩、画一画
Playing and painting

跟着妮妮和杰瑞
做送给朋友的
礼物

Follow Nini and Jerry to make gifts for your friends.

杰瑞的画
Jerry's painting

恐龙

妮妮的手工
Nini's handcraft

想一想、说一说
Thinking and talking

与妮妮和杰瑞一起想一想
Think with Nini and Jerry:
你认识的哪些人是龙年出生的?
他们是什么星座?
Who do you know was born in the Year of the Dragon? What are their astrological signs?

龙年的年份
The Year of the Dragon
1904年、1916年、
1928年、1940年、
1952年、1964年、
1976年、1988年、
2000年、2012年。

龙年出生的名人
Celebrities born in the Year of the Dragon:
朱元璋、邓小平、
巴金、约翰·列侬、
詹姆斯·瓦特。
Zhu Yuanzhang (the first emperor of Ming Dynasty), Deng Xiaoping (general leader of China's market economy reform), Ba Jin (a famous Chinese writer), John Lennon, James G. Watt.

与妮妮和杰瑞一起比赛
Compete with Nini and Jerry:
说出与"龙"
有关的词语或
成语。
Say the words or proverbs related with the word "Long (Dragon)".

A calligrapher born in the Year of the Dragon

《鸭头丸帖》

王献之（344—386），东晋书法家、诗人、画家，与其父王羲之并称"二王"。《鸭头丸帖》是王献之行草的代表作，共15字，全帖笔画劲利灵动，风神散逸，断连结合，疏密相间。整幅字一气呵成，用墨枯润有致，展现出书写的节奏起伏和气韵的自然变化。

Wang Xianzhi (344—386), was a calligrapher, poet and painter of the Eastern Jin Dynasty, who was regarded as "Two Masters" with his father Wang Xizhi. *Ya Tou Wan Tie* is the representative work of Wang Xianzhi's cursive handwriting, including 15 characters. The strokes are sometimes vigorous and vivid in an elegant and loose style, sometimes coherent and sometimes broken, alternate in density. The whole work was completed in one breath and the ink was strewn with the right strength, presenting the fluctuation of the writing rhythm and natural variation of artistic conception.

She
蛇 Snake

The story of Snake

Snake also participated in the 12 Chinese zodiacs river-crossing selection competition. Snake used to have feet. However, as he exerted himself to the maximum in the competition, all his feet were broken. In the end, he got the sixth place in the competition, behind Dragon.

The characteristics of people who were born in the Year of the Snake: they are focused and responsible; they are clever, handy/skilled, keen and intelligent; they have an abundance of energy and they are easy-going and cheerful.

蛇的故事

蛇也积极参加了生肖选拔渡河比赛。它本来是有脚的，但是由于在比赛过程中跑得太卖力，把脚都跑断了，最后它获得了比赛的第六名，排在龙的后面。

生肖为蛇的人性格特点：专心致志，认真负责；心灵手巧，思路敏捷；精力充沛，随和开朗。

跟着妮妮学一学
Learning calligraphy with Nini

篆书 (zhuan shu) | Seal script

"巳"字从篆书字形上看像一个还没有伸出胳膊的婴儿的形状。本义指在胎包中生长的小儿。现指地支的第六位。

The character of "巳(si)" in seal script looks like the shape of a baby who does not stretch his arms out yet. Its original meaning indicates the little baby who is still growing in its embryo. It is also used to indicate the sixth place of Earthly Branches (Dizhi).

"蛇"字从篆书字形上看像一种身体圆细而长、有鳞无爪的动物，贴着地面蜿蜒前行。

The character of "蛇(she)" in seal script looks like an animal that has a round, slim and long body with scales but not claws and closely winds its way against the ground.

扫描右侧二维码，让我们一起来欣赏"蛇"字的动画故事吧！
Let's scan the QR code on the right to enjoy the animation story of the Character "蛇".

扫描右侧二维码，一起来学习它们的基本写法吧！

Let's scan the QR code on the right to watch the videos to learn how to write the characters.

 跟着杰瑞写一写
Practicing calligraphy with Jerry

楷书 (kai shu) | Regular script

  フ コ 巴

  丨 冂 口 中 虫 虫 虫ˊ 虫ˋ
  虫宀 虫它 蛇

45

玩一玩、画一画
Playing and painting

跟着妮妮和杰瑞做送给朋友的
礼物

Follow Nini and Jerry to make gifts for your friends.

杰瑞的画
Jerry's painting

妮妮的手工
Nini's handcraft

想一想、说一说
Thinking and talking

与妮妮和杰瑞一起想一想
Think with Nini and Jerry:
你认识的哪些人是蛇年出生的？
他们是什么星座？
Who do you know was born in the Year of the Snake? What are their astrological signs?

蛇年的年份
The Year of the Snake
1905年、1917年、
1929年、1941年、
1953年、1965年、
1977年、1989年、
2001年、2013年。

蛇年出生的名人
Celebrities born in the Year of the Snake:
鲁迅、毛泽东、
尼古拉·哥白尼、
富兰克林·罗斯福、
毕加索。
Lu Xun (a philosopher and literator), Mao Zedong (a founder of the Chinese Communist Party), Nicholas Copernicus, Franklin Roosevelt, Picasso.

与妮妮和杰瑞一起比赛
Compete with Nini and Jerry:
说出与"蛇"有关的词语或成语。
Say the words or proverbs related with the word "She (Snake)".

A calligrapher born in the Year of the Snake

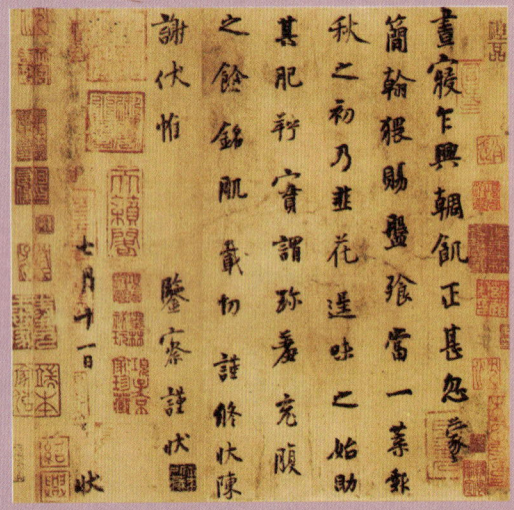

《韭花帖》

杨凝式（873—954），唐末五代时期宰相、书法家，书法史上承唐启宋的重要人物。代表作《韭花帖》点画生动妍丽，顾盼有致；结构端庄温雅，平中寓奇。字间与行间的布白宽疏、散朗，疏密有致，气脉贯通，营造出萧散闲适、自然天成的文人气。

Yang Ningshi (873—954), was a prime minister and calligrapher in the late Tang Dynasty and Five Dynasties, who was regarded as an important figure in the history of calligraphy during the transition of Tang and Song dynasties. His representative work *Leek Flower Tie* is vivid and exquisite in strokes with subtle links. The structures of characters are dignified and gentle with beauty hidden in the blank. The blank space between the characters and lines is dynamically left out, indicating the spirit of a leisure and unpretentious gentle scholar.

Ma 马 Horse

The story of Horse

Goat and Horse were good friends. They participated the 12 Chinese zodiacs river-crossing selection competition together and helped each other in the competition. They were polite to each other and got to the finish line at almost the same time. Horse was just in front of Goat and finished the race in seventh place.

The characteristics of people who were born in the Year of the Horse: they are full of energy and resolute; they maintain a clear sense of good and evil and they are upright and passionate; they are eloquent, fearless and they move forward without hesitation.

马的故事

　　羊和马是一对好朋友,它们一起参加了渡河比赛。它们在比赛中互相帮助,互相谦让,几乎同时到达了终点,马在羊的前面,排在第七位。

生肖为马的人性格特点　精力旺盛,刚毅果断;善恶分明,耿直热情;能言善辩,不怕困难,勇往直前。

跟着妮妮学一学
Learning calligraphy with Nini

篆书 (zhuan shu) | Seal script

"午"字从篆书字形上看像杵棒上有两个横结，横结的作用是增加杵棒在臼中舂米的摩擦力。本义指有两个横结的舂米棒，后引申为抵触、违反。又为地支的第七位。

The character of "午(wu)" in seal script looks like a pestle with two horizontal knots. The function of the knots is to add the friction to the pestle when it is pounding rice in the mortar. Its original meaning is the pestle with two horizontal knots and later is extended to the meaning of contradiction and violation. It is also used to indicate the seventh place of Earthly Branches(Dizhi).

"马"字从篆书字形上看像长脸、大眼、鬃毛飞扬、长尾有蹄的动物形象。本义指一种善跑的哺乳动物，可供人骑或拉东西。

The character of "马(ma)" in seal script looks like the image of an animal that has a long face, big eyes, flying hair, a long tail and hooves. Its original meaning is a kind of mammal that is good at running and can be used by man for riding or pulling things.

扫描右侧二维码，让我们一起来欣赏"马"字的动画故事吧！

Let's scan the QR code on the right to enjoy the animation story of the Character "马".

扫描右侧二维码，一起来学习它们的基本写法吧！

Let's scan the QR code on the right to watch the videos to learn how to write the characters.

跟着杰瑞写一写
Practicing calligraphy with Jerry

楷书（kai shu）| Regular script

丿 𠂉 𠂊 午

丨 厂 厂 F 𠃜 馬 馬
馬 馬 馬

玩一玩、画一画
Playing and painting

跟着妮妮和杰瑞
做送给朋友的
礼物

Follow Nini and Jerry to make gifts for your friends.

杰瑞的画
Jerry's painting

妮妮的手工
Nini's handcraft

想一想、说一说
Thinking and talking

与妮妮和杰瑞一起想一想
Think with Nini and Jerry:
你认识的哪些人是马年出生的？他们是什么星座？
Who do you know was born in the Year of the Horse? What are their astrological signs?

马年的年份
The Year of the Horse
1906年、1918年、1930年、1942年、1954年、1966年、1978年、1990年、2002年、2014年。

马年出生的名人
Celebrities born in the Year of the Horse:
成吉思汗、康熙皇帝、梅兰芳、列宁。
Genghis Khan (the Mongol conqueror), Emperor Kang-xi (an emperor of Qing Dynasty), Mei Lanfang (a famous performing artist of Beijing Opera), Vladimir Lenin.

与妮妮和杰瑞一起比赛
Compete with Nini and Jerry:
说出与"马"有关的词语或成语。
Say the words or proverbs related with the word "Ma (Horse)".

A calligrapher born in the Year of the Horse

《玄秘塔碑》

柳公权（778—865），唐代书法家、诗人，以楷书著称，"楷书四大家"之一。"柳体"楷书集各家之长，融汇新意，独树一帜，以骨力劲健见长，后世有"颜筋柳骨"的美誉。代表作《玄秘塔碑》点画丰富多变，行笔挺劲舒长，通篇方折峻整，清劲挺拔。

Liu Gongquan (778—865), was a calligrapher and poet of Tang Dynasty, one of the "Four Masters of Regular Script" and was famous for his regular script. Liu-style regular script was inspired by the works of different masters and was further developed into a distinctive style. Liu's calligraphy is vigorous and strong, which is praised as "Yan Jin Liu Gu" style in later generations. His representative work, *Stele of Xuanmi Pagoda* has changeable dots and long strokes, with a grim, neat, clear and vigorous style.

Yang
羊 Goat

The story of Goat

Goat and Horse were good friends. They participated the 12 Chinese zodiacs river-crossing selection competition together and helped each other in the competition. They were polite to each other and got to the finish line at almost the same time. Horse was lined seventh while Goat was lined in the eighth place.

The characteristics of people who were born in the Year of the Goat: they are kind and generous; they are docile and patient; they try to stay out of trouble and have a good relationship with others.

羊的故事

羊和它的好朋友马一起参加了生肖选拔比赛，它们在比赛中互相协助，互相谦让。最终马排在了第七位，羊紧随其后排在了第八位。

生肖为羊的人性格特点　善良，宽容；性情温和，有耐心；不惹是非，善于与人相处。

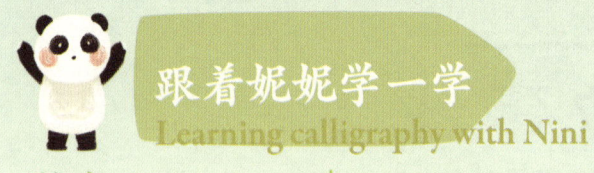

跟着妮妮学一学
Learning calligraphy with Nini
篆书 (zhuan shu) | Seal script

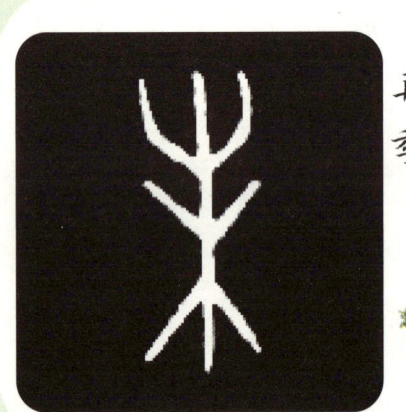

"未"字从篆书字形上看像是在树木的枝杈上部再加一重枝桠，形容树上枝叶重叠的样子。本义指夏季果树枝叶茂盛，还没结果。引申为没有。又指地支的第八位。

The character of "未(wei)" in seal script looks like adding another bunch of branches on the top of one bunch of branch describing the way the branches of a overlap. Its original meaning is a summer tree that has prosperous tree leaves, although it is not fruiting. It is also extended as "none". It is also used to indicate the eighth place of Earthly Branches(Dizhi).

"羊"字从篆书字形上看像两角弯曲，两鼻孔在鼻尖上形成"V"形的动物。本义指一种两角弯曲、性情温顺的食草动物。引申为吉利、吉祥。

The character of "羊(yang)" in seal script looks like an animal that has two curly horns and two nostrils forming a shape of "V" on the tip of its nose. Its original meaning is a kind of herbivores that has two curly horns and has a docile temperament. And it is extended as luck and blessing.

扫描右侧二维码，让我们一起来欣赏"羊"字的动画故事吧！
Let's scan the QR code on the right to enjoy the animation story of the Character "羊".

扫描右侧二维码，一起来学习它们的基本写法吧！

Let's scan the QR code on the right to watch the videos to learn how to write the characters.

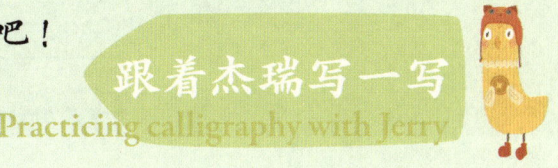

跟着杰瑞写一写
Practicing calligraphy with Jerry

楷书（kai shu）| Regular script

一 二 十 才 未

丶 丷 丷 丷 丷 羊

玩一玩、画一画
Playing and painting

跟着妮妮和杰瑞做送给朋友的
礼物

Follow Nini and Jerry to make gifts for your friends.

杰瑞的画
Jerry's painting

米羊

妮妮的手工
Nini's handcraft

想一想、说一说
Thinking and talking

与妮妮和杰瑞一起想一想
Think with Nini and Jerry:
你认识的哪些人是羊年出生的？
他们是什么星座？
Who do you know was born in the Year of the Goat? What are their astrological signs?

羊年的年份
The Year of the Goat
1907年、1919年、
1931年、1943年、
1955年、1967年、
1979年、1991年、
2003年、2015年。

羊年出生的名人
Celebrities born in the Year of the Goat:
曹操、岳飞、
马克·吐温、
爱迪生、
比尔·盖茨。
Cao Cao (a central figure of the Three Kingdoms Period), Yue Fei (a military general of the Southern Song Dynasty), Mark Twain, Thomas Alva Edison, Bill Gates.

与妮妮和杰瑞一起比赛
Compete with Nini and Jerry:
说出与"羊"有关的词语或成语。
Say the words or proverbs related with the word "Yang (Goat)".

A calligrapher born in the Year of the Goat

《草书七言诗》

傅山（1607—1684），明清之际道家思想家、书法家、医学家。他五种书体兼备，尤其擅长连绵大草，豪迈不羁，意到笔随，把草书推向了极致。《草书七言诗》一气呵成，心手两畅，墨色跌宕，潇洒奇逸。傅山主张书法学习以古法为上，但反对泥古不化。

Fu Shan (1607—1684), was a Taoist thinker, calligrapher and medical scientist between Ming and Qing dynasties. He was good at five scripts, especially the continuous wild cursive script. His style was bold and spontaneous, pushing the cursive script to the extreme. *Poem in Cursive Script* was done with consistency, indicating the harmony of the writer's hands and mind. The ink color fluctuated with a natural, unrestrained and amazing style. Fu Shan advocated the study of calligraphy should refer to the ancient method, but shouldn't follow the old script without changes.

Hou 猴 Monkey

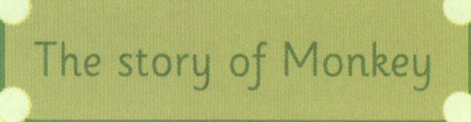
The story of Monkey

Monkey remained last in the 12 Chinese zodiacs river-crossing selection competition. When he almost arrived at the finish line, using his jumping skills, Monkey jumped ahead and grabbed the tree branches along the river bank and swung ahead. He passed several opponents to be able to arrive at the finish line right after Goat and was ranked as the ninth place.

The characteristics of people who were born in the Year of the Monkey: they are smart, swift and has a strong initiative; they are talented and aren't willing to be restrained; they get along well with others and they are good at socializing with others.

猴的故事

　　猴子在渡河比赛中一直落在最后，快到终点时，它凭着自己会跳的本领，纵身一跃，拉起河岸边大树的枝条向前荡去，赶超了好几名对手，最终紧随羊的后面到达终点，排在了第九位。

生肖为猴的人性格特点　聪明、灵巧，有进取心；多才多艺，不受拘束；能与人融洽相处，善于应酬。

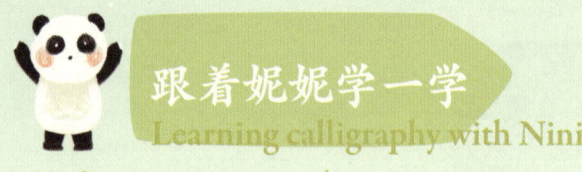

跟着妮妮学一学
Learning calligraphy with Nini
篆书 (zhuan shu) | Seal script

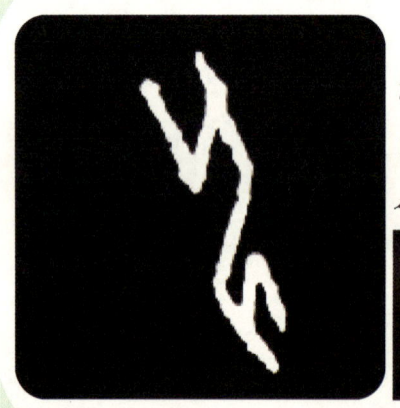 

"申"字从篆书字形上看像神秘而令人惊恐的、朝着各个方向开裂的闪电。本义指雨天的闪电。引申为伸张、扩展。又指地支的第九位。

The character of "申(shen)" in seal script looks like a mysterious but horrifying lightening that splashes to all directions. Its original meaning is the lightening on a rainy day and was extended to mean "stretch" and "expand". It is also used to indicate the ninth place of Earthly Branches (Dizhi).

"猴"字从篆书字形上看分为两部分,左边是形旁,看上去像一只长尾巴的小猴子,右边"侯"是声旁,代表这个字的读音。本义指一种长臂猿。

The character of "猴 (hou)" in seal script can be separated into two parts in its shape. The left part is its semantic sign which looks like a little monkey with a long tail. The right part "侯 (hou)" is its phonetic sign. Its original meaning is a kind of gibbon mentioned in ancient literature.

扫描右侧二维码,让我们一起来欣赏"猴"字的动画故事吧!
Let's scan the QR code on the right to enjoy the animation story of the Character "猴".

扫描右侧二维码，一起来学习它们的基本写法吧！

Let's scan the QR code on the right to watch the videos to learn how to write the characters.

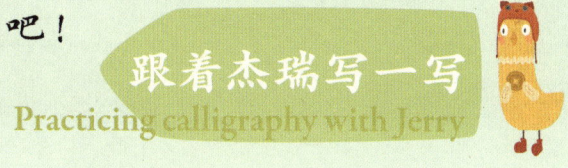

跟着杰瑞写一写

Practicing calligraphy with Jerry

楷书（kai shu）| Regular script

丨 冂 冋 日 申

丿 亅 犭 犭 犭 犭 犭 犭 犭 猴 猴

69

玩一玩、画一画
Playing and painting

跟着妮妮和杰瑞
做送给朋友的
礼物

Follow Nini and Jerry to make gifts for your friends.

杰瑞的画
Jerry's painting

妮妮的手工
Nini's handcraft

想一想、说一说
Thinking and talking

与妮妮和杰瑞一起想一想
Think with Nini and Jerry:
你认识的哪些人
是猴年出生的?
他们是什么星座?

Who do you know was born in the Year of the Monkey? What are their astrological signs?

猴年的年份
The Year of the Monkey
1908年、1920年、
1932年、1944年、
1956年、1968年、
1980年、1992年、
2004年、2016年。

猴年出生的名人
Celebrities born in the Year of the Monkey:
曹植、武则天、辛弃疾、
乔治·戈登·拜伦、
查尔斯·狄更斯、
达·芬奇。

Cao Zhi (a prince of the state of Wei of the Three kingdoms Period), Empress Wu Zetian (the only empress regnant of China), Xin Qiji (a poet of the Southern Song Dynasty), George Gordon Byron, Charles Dickens, Leonardo da Vinci.

与妮妮和杰瑞一起比赛
Compete with Nini and Jerry:
说出与"猴"
有关的词语或
成语。

Say the words or proverbs related with the word "Hou (Monkey)".

A calligrapher born in the Year of the Monkey

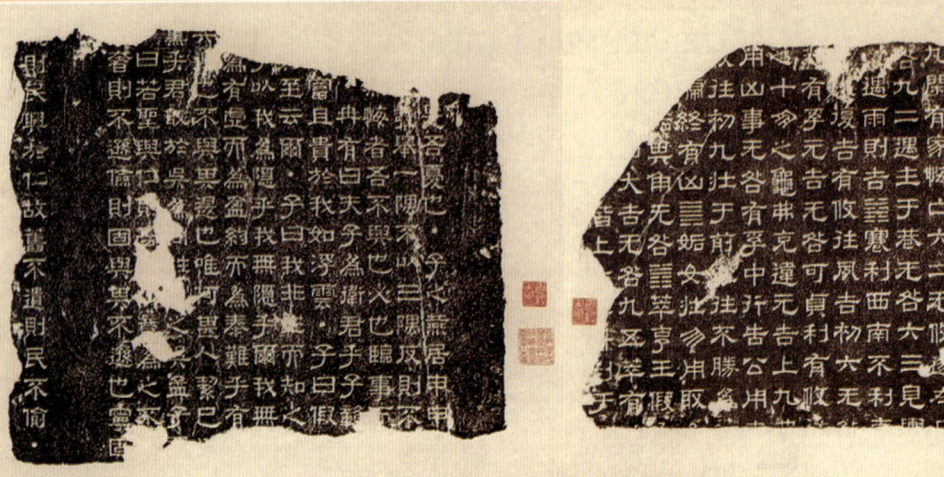

《熹平石经》

蔡邕（133—192），东汉名臣、文学家、书法家。尤以隶书造诣最高，他所创的"飞白"书体，对后世影响甚大。《熹平石经》点画俯仰，变化自如，字形方正，结构精严端庄，气势恢宏，是当时通行的标准字体。他强调书法应取法自然，表现美妙的姿态。

Cai Yong (133—192), was a famous official, literator and calligrapher of the Eastern Han Dynasty. His highest achievement was especially accomplished in clerical script and the "Fei Bai" style created by him had a great influence on later generations. *Xiping Stone Classics* were the prevailing standard font at that time. The strokes change freely; the words are well balanced with an elegant structure, indicating magnificent momentum. Cai Yong emphasized that calligraphy should be drawn from nature, manifesting beautiful gestures.

Ji
鸡 Rooster

The story of Rooster

As the legend goes, before the Big Race, dragons did not have horns while on the other hand, roosters had a pair of beautiful horns. Dragon wanted to stand out in the Big Race and so he persuaded Rooster to lend him his horns by telling the rooster that he was pretty enough and didn't need the horns. Rooster was so happy to hear the flattery that he lent his horns to Dragon and asked him to return them once the race finished. After the race, Rooster got the 10th place while Dragon got the fifth place. Dragon went to the seaside and saw himself in the sea that he was much more pretty with the horns than before. As a result, he decided not to return the horns. He chose to disappear from man's world to avoid Rooster. Rooster was so indignant at this that he shouted at the sea: "Quickly return the horns to me! Quickly return the horns to me!" very early every morning since then.

The characteristics of people who were born in the Year of the Rooster: they are energetic and good at talking; they are decisive, keen, and they tend to flaunt themselves and desire to amaze the world with a single brilliant feat.

鸡的故事

据说生肖选拔之前龙是没有犄角的，而鸡有一对美丽的犄角。龙为了让自己在比赛中更显风姿，就对鸡说，鸡已经很漂亮了，用不着犄角，请鸡借给它。鸡一听龙的称赞，十分高兴，就把犄角借给了龙，并嘱咐龙比赛结束后按时还给它。比赛结束了，鸡得了第十名，而龙是第五名。龙来到了大海边，看到有犄角的自己比以前漂亮多了，就不准备归还犄角了。为了躲鸡，它从此就从人间消失了。鸡气愤极了，从此以后天天一大早就起来对着大海喊："快还我！快还我！"

生肖为鸡的人性格特点　精力充沛，善于言谈；果断、敏锐、有表现欲，渴望一鸣惊人。

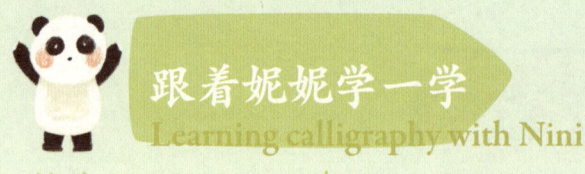

跟着妮妮学一学
Learning calligraphy with Nini

篆书 (zhuan shu) | Seal script

"酉"字从篆书字形上看像一个尖底的坛子，中间加一横，表示坛子里有酒。本义指酒。又指地支的第十位。

The character of "酉(you)" in seal script looks like a sharp-bottomed jar. Adding one horizontal stroke inside the character indicates that there is alcohol inside of the jar. Its original meaning is alcohol. It is also used to indicate the tenth place of Earthly Branches (Dizhi).

"鸡"字从篆书字形上看由两部分组成。左边表示用绳子系住或套住，右边像有冠、长尾的大鸟。本义指古人从林野抓捕后用绳子系住驯养在家的飞禽。

The character of "鸡(ji)" in seal script can be separated into two parts in its shape. The left part indicates the action of tying or holding up something with a rope while the right part looks like a huge crested bird with a long tail. Its original meaning is the birds that were captured by the ancestors from the woods and then were tied up with a rope and domesticated at home.

扫描右侧二维码，让我们一起来欣赏"鸡"字的动画故事吧！

Let's scan the QR code on the right to enjoy the animation story of the Character "鸡".

扫描右侧二维码，一起来学习它们的基本写法吧！

Let's scan the QR code on the right to watch the videos to learn how to write the characters.

跟着杰瑞写一写

Practicing calligraphy with Jerry

楷书 (kai shu) | Regular script

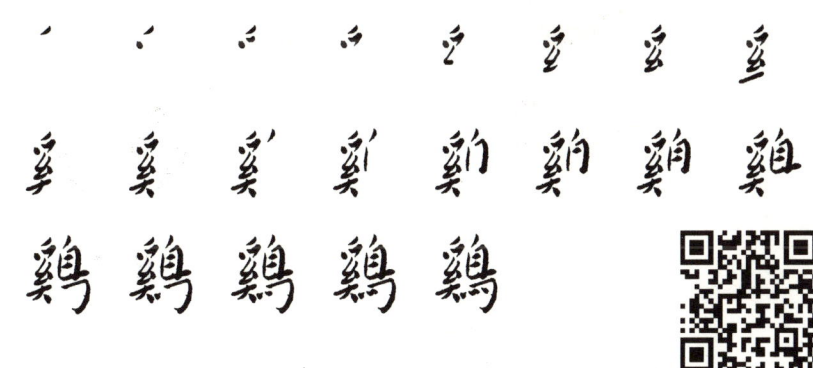

77

玩一玩、画一画
Playing and painting

跟着妮妮和杰瑞
做送给朋友的
礼物

Follow Nini and Jerry to make gifts for your friends.

杰瑞的画
Jerry's painting

妮妮的手工
Nini's handcraft

想一想、说一说
Thinking and talking

与妮妮和杰瑞一起想一想
Think with Nini and Jerry:
你认识的哪些人是鸡年出生的?
他们是什么星座?
Who do you know was born in the Year of the Rooster? What are their astrological signs?

鸡年的年份
The Year of the Rooster
1909年、1921年、
1933年、1945年、
1957年、1969年、
1981年、1993年、
2005年、2017年。

鸡年出生的名人
Celebrities born in the Year of the Rooster:
汉武帝刘彻、
颜真卿、王安石、
亚里士多德、
弗朗西斯·培根、
泰戈尔。
Emperor Liu Che (an emperor of Han Dynasty), Yan Zhenqing (a Chinese calligrapher), Wang Anshi (a politician and literator of the Northern Song Dynasty), Aristotle, Francis Bacon, and Tagore.

与妮妮和杰瑞一起比赛
Compete with Nini and Jerry:
说出与"鸡"有关的词语或成语。
Say the words or proverbs related with the word "Ji (Rooster)".

A calligrapher born in the Year of the Rooster

《自书告身帖》

颜真卿(709—784)，唐朝名臣、书法家，"楷书四大家"之一。《自书告身帖》是其楷书代表作之一，端庄朴厚，苍劲有力，结体宽博而气势恢宏，骨力道劲而气概凛然。这种风格体现了大唐帝国繁盛的气象，并与他高尚的人格契合，是书法美与人格美的完美结合。

Yan Zhenqing (709—784), a famous official and calligrapher of Tang Dynasty, one of "Four Masters of Regular Script". *Certificate of Appointment* is one of the representative works of Yan's regular script. This work boasts the dignified and vigorous feature with broad structures, magnificent momentum and powerful strokes. Such style reflects the prosperity of Tang Dynasty and Yan Zhenqing's noble personality, which is a perfect combination of the beauty in calligraphy and personality.

Gou
狗 Dog

The story of Dog

Although Dog also participated in the 12 Chinese zodiacs river-crossing selection competition, he was playing around during the competition and he got slowed down and was left behind by other animals. Because of this, he was ranked in the 11th place after Rooster.

The characteristics of people who were born in the Year of the Dog: they are determined and loyal; they have a strong sense of justice and they are brave; they are agile, smart and friendly.

狗的故事

虽然狗也参加了生肖选拔比赛,但它在比赛过程中非常贪玩,走走停停,以至于耽误了时间,被别的动物甩在身后,最后它排在了鸡的后面,位列第十一。

生肖为狗的人性格特点:意志坚定,忠诚可靠;正直、侠义;敏捷,聪明,友好。

跟着妮妮学一学
Learning calligraphy with Nini
篆书 (zhuan shu) | Seal script

"戌"字从篆书字形上看像一把斧子。本义指战斧。又指地支的第十一位。

The character of "戌(xu)" in seal script looks like an axe. Its original meaning is battleaxe. It is also used to indicate the eleventh place of Earthly Branches (Dizhi).

"狗"字从篆书字形上看可以分为两部分。左边为形符，右边为声符。指一种听觉、嗅觉特别灵敏，行动机警的哺乳动物。

The character of "狗(gou)" in seal script can be separated into two parts in its shape. The left part is the semantic sign while the right part is the phonetic sign. Its original meaning is a kind of mammals that has especially agile hearing and strong sense of smell while acts intelligently.

扫描右侧二维码，让我们一起来欣赏"狗"字的动画故事吧！
Let's scan the QR code on the right to enjoy the animation story of the Character "狗".

扫描右侧二维码，一起来学习它们的基本写法吧！

Let's scan the QR code on the right to watch the videos to learn how to write the characters.

跟着杰瑞写一写

Practicing calligraphy with Jerry

楷书（kai shu）| Regular script

一 厂 厂 F 成 成 成

丿 犭 犭 犭 狗 狗 狗 狗

玩一玩、画一画
Playing and painting

跟着妮妮和杰瑞做送给朋友的 **礼物**

Follow Nini and Jerry to make gifts for your friends.

杰瑞的画
Jerry's painting

戌狗

妮妮的手工
Nini's handcraft

想一想、说一说
Thinking and talking

与妮妮和杰瑞一起想一想
Think with Nini and Jerry:
你认识的哪些人是狗年出生的？
他们是什么星座？
Who do you know was born in the Year of the Dog? What are their astrological signs?

狗年的年份
The Year of the Dog
1910年、1922年、
1934年、1946年、
1958年、1970年、
1982年、1994年、
2006年、2018年。

狗年出生的名人
Celebrities born in the Year of the Dog:
孙权、朱熹、周恩来、
阿基米德、
本杰明·富兰克林、
迈克尔·杰克逊。
Sun Quan (founder of the state of Wu of the Three Kingdoms Period), Zhu Xi (a Confucian scholar of Song Dynasty), Zhou Enlai (the first Premier of the People's Republic of China), Archimedes, Benjamin Franklin, and Michael Jackson.

与妮妮和杰瑞一起比赛
Compete with Nini and Jerry:
说出与"狗"
有关的词语或
成语。
Say the words or proverbs related with the word "Gou (Dog)".

A calligrapher born in the Year of the Dog

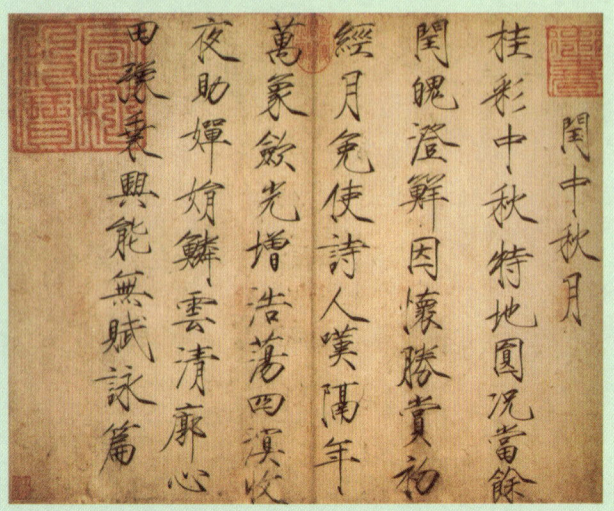

《闰中秋月诗帖》

赵佶（1082—1135），宋朝第八位皇帝，书画家。其书法瘦直挺拔，横画收笔带钩，竖画收笔带点，撇如匕首，捺如切刀，竖钩细长。有些连笔如游丝行空，已接近行书，号称"瘦金体"。《闰中秋月诗帖》用笔劲健舒展，结体飘逸优雅，是"瘦金书"中风格偏于柔美的作品。

Zhao Ji (1082—1135), the eighth emperor of Song Dynasty, was also a calligrapher and painter. His calligraphy is thin and straight, whose horizontal strokes pose a slender hook, vertical strokes with a point, left-falling stroke like a dagger, right-falling stroke like a knife, and with slender vertical hooks. The continuous drawing strokes are close to the running script, named as "Shou Jin Style". The brushwork in *Intercalary Mid-Autumn Month Post* is vigorous and unrestrained with elegant and ethereal structure, which belongs to a mellow "Shou Jin Style".

Zhu
猪 Pig

The story of Pig

Now there was only one place left in the 12 Chinese zodiacs selection competition. Everyone was waiting at the finish line in a most flattering state of expectancy to see who was the next to arrive. "Pig is coming! Pig is coming!", some small animals shouted. Pig was sweating profusely. He snorted and then said, "I'm starving to death. Is there anything to eat?" "Haha haha…" Everyone bursted into laughter. Although Pig was ranked as the last place in the 12 Chinese zodiacs, at least he made his name on the list.

The characteristics of people who were born in the Year of the Pig: they are kind, sincere, passionate and sympathetic; they are energetic, friendly, cheerful and optimistic.

猪的故事

十二生肖只剩下最后一个名额了,大家都伸长脖子期待着下一个到达终点的参赛者。"猪来了!猪来了!"小动物们叫喊起来。只见猪满头大汗,喘着气说:"饿死我了,这里有没有好吃的东西?"大家哈哈大笑。猪虽然排在了十二生肖的最后一位,但也总算是挤进了生肖的行列。

生肖为猪的人性格特点　善良真挚、热情、有同情心;精力旺盛,待人友好,开朗乐观。

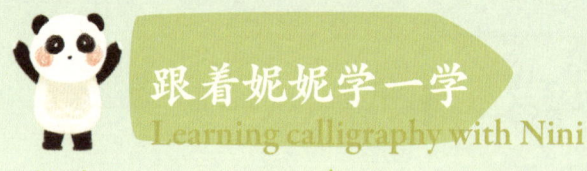

跟着妮妮学一学
Learning calligraphy with Nini

篆书 (zhuan shu) | Seal script

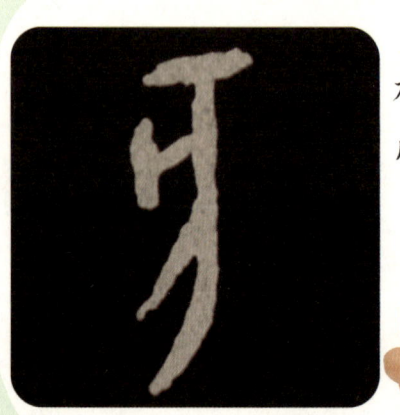

"亥"字从篆书字形上看表示在人的颈部加上一个短横,意为喉咙发出声音。本义为幼儿喉部发出的"呵呵"的笑声。又指地支的第十二位。

The character of "亥(hai)" in seal script looks like adding a short horizontal stroke on someone's neck, indicating the sound coming from the throat. Its original meaning is babies' cackle of laughter coming from the throat. It is also used to indicate the twelfth place of Earthly Branches (Dizhi).

"猪"字从篆书字形上看可以分为两部分,左边"豕"为形符,意为猪。右边"者"为声符。

The character of "猪(zhu)" in seal script can be separated into two parts in its shape. The left part is the semantic sign "豕(shi)" which means pig, while the right part "者(zhe)" is its phonetic sign.

扫描右侧二维码,让我们一起来欣赏"猪"字的动画故事吧!
Let's scan the QR code on the right to enjoy the animation story of the Character "猪".

扫描右侧二维码，一起来学习它们的基本写法吧！

Let's scan the QR code on the right to watch the videos to learn how to write the characters.

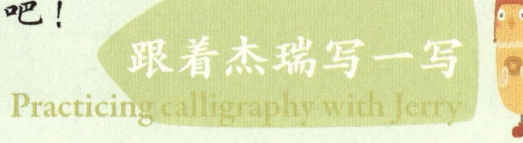

楷书 (kai shu) | Regular script

丶 亠 宀 ナ 灰 灰

丿 孑 孑 犭 犭 犭 犲 狣 猪 猪 猪

玩一玩、画一画
Playing and painting

跟着妮妮和杰瑞
做送给朋友的
礼物

Follow Nini and Jerry to make gifts for your friends.

杰瑞的画
Jerry's painting

亥猪

妮妮的手工
Nini's handcraft

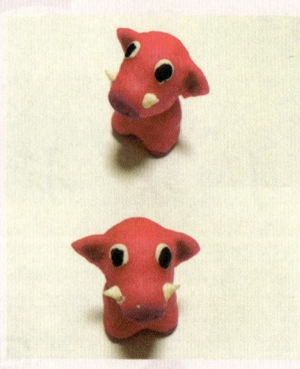

想一想、说一说
Thinking and talking

与妮妮和杰瑞一起想一想
Think with Nini and Jerry:
你认识的哪些人是猪年出生的？他们是什么星座？
Who do you know was born in the Year of the Pig? What are their astrological signs?

猪年的年份
The Year of the Pig
1911年、1923年、1935年、1947年、1959年、1971年、1983年、1995年、2007年、2019年。

猪年出生的名人
Celebrities born in the Year of the Pig:
王羲之、赵匡胤、忽必烈、海明威、罗纳德·威尔逊·里根。

Wang Xizhi (a famous calligrapher of the Eastern Jin Dynasty), Zhao Kuangyin (founder of the Northern Song Dynasty), Kublai Khan (founder of Yuan Dynasty), Ernest Miller Hemingway, Ronald Wilson Reagan.

与妮妮和杰瑞一起比赛
Compete with Nini and Jerry:
说出与"猪"有关的词语或成语。
Say the words or proverbs related with the word "Zhu (Pig)".

A calligrapher born in the Year of the Pig

Lushan Cottage

Deng Shiru (1743—1805), was a seal engraver and calligrapher of Qing Dynasty. His seal script is slightly square, close to the wall tiles and steles of Qin and Han dynasties. He creatively integrated the brushwork of clerical script into the seal script, and wrote boldly and freely with a long and soft brush, so as to enrich the strokes of the seal script. *Lushan Cottage* is a work of Deng's in his later years. The strokes are round and heavy with amagnificent momentum. The whole composition is steadily and tidy while the structures are strong and determined.

《白氏草堂记》

邓石如（1743—1805），清代篆刻家、书法家。篆书字体微方，接近秦汉瓦当和汉碑额。他创造性地将隶书笔法融入篆书，大胆地用长锋软毫，提按起伏，以丰富篆书的用笔。《白氏草堂记》是其晚年作品，线条圆涩厚重，雄浑苍茫，行气整饬工稳，体势森严刚毅。

后记

"书法小联合国"书法文化特色教材《风调雨顺：春夏秋冬》自2017年出版以来，得到了各国国际汉语教育工作者的充分肯定，目前已被翻译成多国语种。第八任联合国秘书长、博鳌亚洲论坛理事长潘基文先生专程为教材写了推荐词："周斌教授编写的《风调雨顺：春夏秋冬》——一本让全世界人民都可来参与书法与文化学习的好书。"

非常有幸，作为中国古代气象文化的入门教材，该书一出版就被耶鲁大学森林与环境学院（Yale School of Forestry & Environmental Studies）收藏并用于教学与科研。而后，在向世界各地不断推广的过程中，该书还被曾经是人类文明中心的亚历山大图书馆收藏。

在各方的鼓励与支持下，我与我的团队在鼠年为大家奉献一本新的教材《十二生肖》。

其实这项构思在十年前就形成了，此次出版是对世界各地使用的上一版教材的进一步优化，以适应世界各国学习中华文化的需要。

"书法小联合国"书法文化特色系列教材编写的目标是：既尊重不同国家的文化习俗，又努力做到精准传播中华文化，把中国故事讲好。

不管你来自哪个国家，每个人都可以找到自己的生肖故事。在教材的最后，我们为大家呈现了十二星座与十二生肖的对照图，以方便读者比较中西文化间的异同。

目前，该教材已在联合国国际学校、美国加德纳小学、上海市金山区第二实验小学等多所中外学校的青少年教学中试用。教材通过讲解汉字的运笔与结构特点，解读汉字文化内涵，来帮助不同文化背景的学生轻松学习中国文化。教材由书法家专门用小楷书写，使之更具中华文化的感染力。通过扫描教材中的二维码，还可以观看书法艺术教学视频，帮助读者在学习生肖文化、书法文化的同时，培养动手能力。

感谢潘基文先生对"书法小联合国"书法文化特色系列教材的鼎力支持,感谢上海交通大学上海交大—南加州大学文化创意产业学院张伟民院长、美国理海大学康妮教授、纽约大学唐力行教授、联合国国际学校孙青倩等老师在教材编写中提出的建议,感谢华东师范大学出版社王焰社长在教材出版过程中的大力支持,相信"书法小联合国"系列教材将会在"中华文化走出去"的过程中发挥积极的作用。

在我55岁生日之际,谨以此书献给我人生中一直给予我鼓励与支持的亲爱的父母与妻子。

周斌于中国书法文化国际传播研究所

2019年11月16日

Postscript

Since 2017, *Season with Timely Breeze and Rain for Crop Raising: Spring, Summer, Fall and Winter*—the textbooks of a special course on calligraphy culture by Junior United Nations of Calligraphy have been highly affirmed by international Chinese language educators all over the world and has so far been translated into multiple languages. Ban Ki-moon, the eighth UN Secretary-General, Chairman of Bo'ao Forum for Asia, has written an endorsement especially for the textbooks: "*Season with Timely Breeze and Rain for Crop Raising: Spring, Summer, Fall and Winter* by Professor Zhou Bin—good books that make people all over the world participate in calligraphy and culture learning."

Fortunately, as a set of Chinese ancient meteorology culture teaching materials, these serials of books have been collected and used as teaching and research materials by Yale School of Forestry & Environmental Studies. Later, these serials of books have also been collected by the library of Alexandria, once the center of human civilization, when they were being promoted to all parts of the world.

With the encouragement and support by all parties, my team and I are presenting a new teaching material to everyone in the Year of the Rat—*12 Chinese Zodiacs*.

As a matter of fact, the conception of this book formed 10 years ago. This publication is a further optimized version based on the last one applied all over the world to meet the need of worldwide Chinese culture learning.

The purpose of compiling the textbooks of a special course on calligraphy culture by Junior United Nations of Calligraphy is not only to respect different countries' culture customs but also to try to precisely broadcast Chinese culture and tell the Chinese story well.

No matter where you are from, everyone can find your own zodiac story in this teaching material. At the end of this teaching material, we present to you the table of the 12 Chinese zodiac signs and the corresponding astrological signs so that our readers can compare the similarities and differences between Chinese and Western cultures.

At present, this teaching material has been on trial by teenagers in multiple Chinese and international schools such as United Nation International School, US Gardener Primary School, Shanghai Jinshan Second Experimental Primary School, etc. This book explains handling of brush on Chinese strokes and the structures of Chinese characters and also interprets their cultural connotations to help students with different cultural background learn Chinese culture easily. This book is specially written by the calligrapher in regular script in small characters to make it more infectious with Chinese culture. By scanning the QR code in the book, readers may also watch the calligraphy teaching videos so as to learn the zodiac culture and calligraphy culture, as well as develop their own calligraphy skills.

    Here I want to extend my sincere gratitude to the former UN Secretary-General, Mr. Ban Ki-moon for his full support of these series of teaching materials on a special course on calligraphy culture by Junior United Nations of Calligraphy. I also want to extend my gratitude to Professor Zhang Weimin from Shanghai Jiao Tong University, Professor Connie from Lehigh University, Professor Tang Lixing from New York University, Mrs. Sun Qingqian from United Nation International School for their pertinent suggestions during the process of compiling these course books. I am also grateful to president of East China Normal University Press, Mrs. Wang Yan, for her substantial support during the publication process. I firmly believe that the publication of *Junior United Nations of Calligraphy* series would play a very positive role in the development of "Chinese culture going global".

    On my 55th birthday, I dedicate this book to my beloved parents and wife, who continuously give me encouragement and support in my life.

Zhou Bin

In Chinese Calligraphy Culture Education and Communication Center

November 16th, 2019

图书在版编目（CIP）数据

十二生肖 / 周斌，周佳楠主编 . —上海：华东师范大学出版社，2020

ISBN 978-7-5760-0141-9

Ⅰ.①十… Ⅱ.①周… ②周… Ⅲ.①汉语－对外汉语教学－语言读物 Ⅳ.① H195.5

中国版本图书馆 CIP 数据核字（2020）第 035429 号

十二生肖

主　　编　周　斌　周佳楠
责任编辑　曹　琛
责任校对　张佳妮
封面设计　刘怡霖

出版发行　华东师范大学出版社
社　　址　上海市中山北路 3663 号 邮编 200062
网　　址　www.ecnupress.com.cn
电　　话　021-60821666　行政传真 021-62572105
客服电话　021-62865537　门市（邮购）电话 021-62869887
地　　址　上海市中山北路 3663 号华东师范大学校内先锋路口
网　　店　http://hdsdcbs.tmall.com

印 刷 者　上海盛通时代印刷有限公司
开　　本　700×1000　12 开
印　　张　13⅔
字　　数　55 千字
版　　次　2020 年 6 月第一版
印　　次　2020 年 6 月第一次
书　　号　ISBN 978-7-5760-0141-9
定　　价　88.00 元
出 版 人　王　焰

（如发现本版图书有印订质量问题，请寄回本社客服中心调换或电话 021-62865537 联系）

十二生肖与十二星座图

The Table of 12 Chinese Zodiac Signs and 12 Astrological Signs

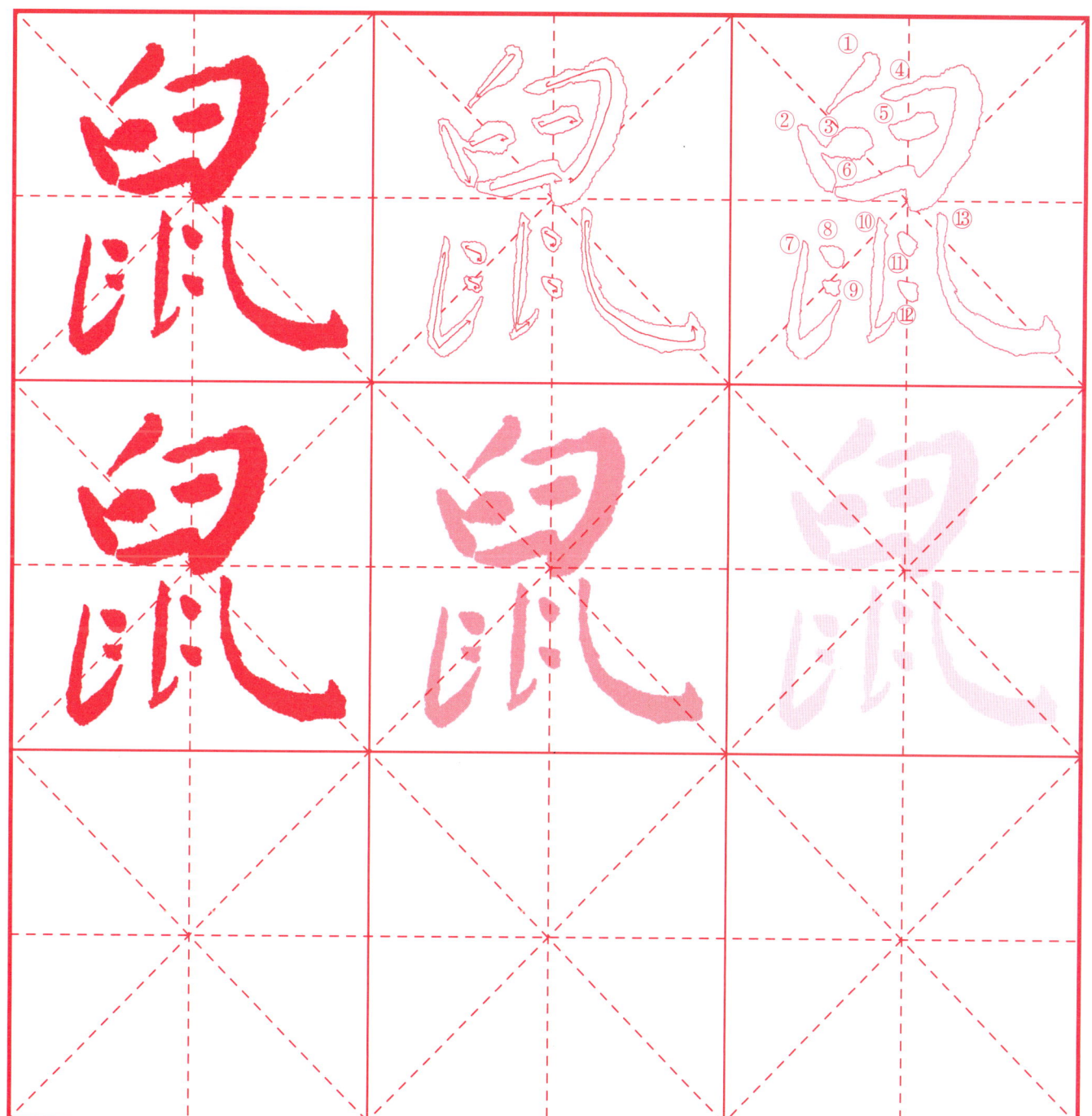

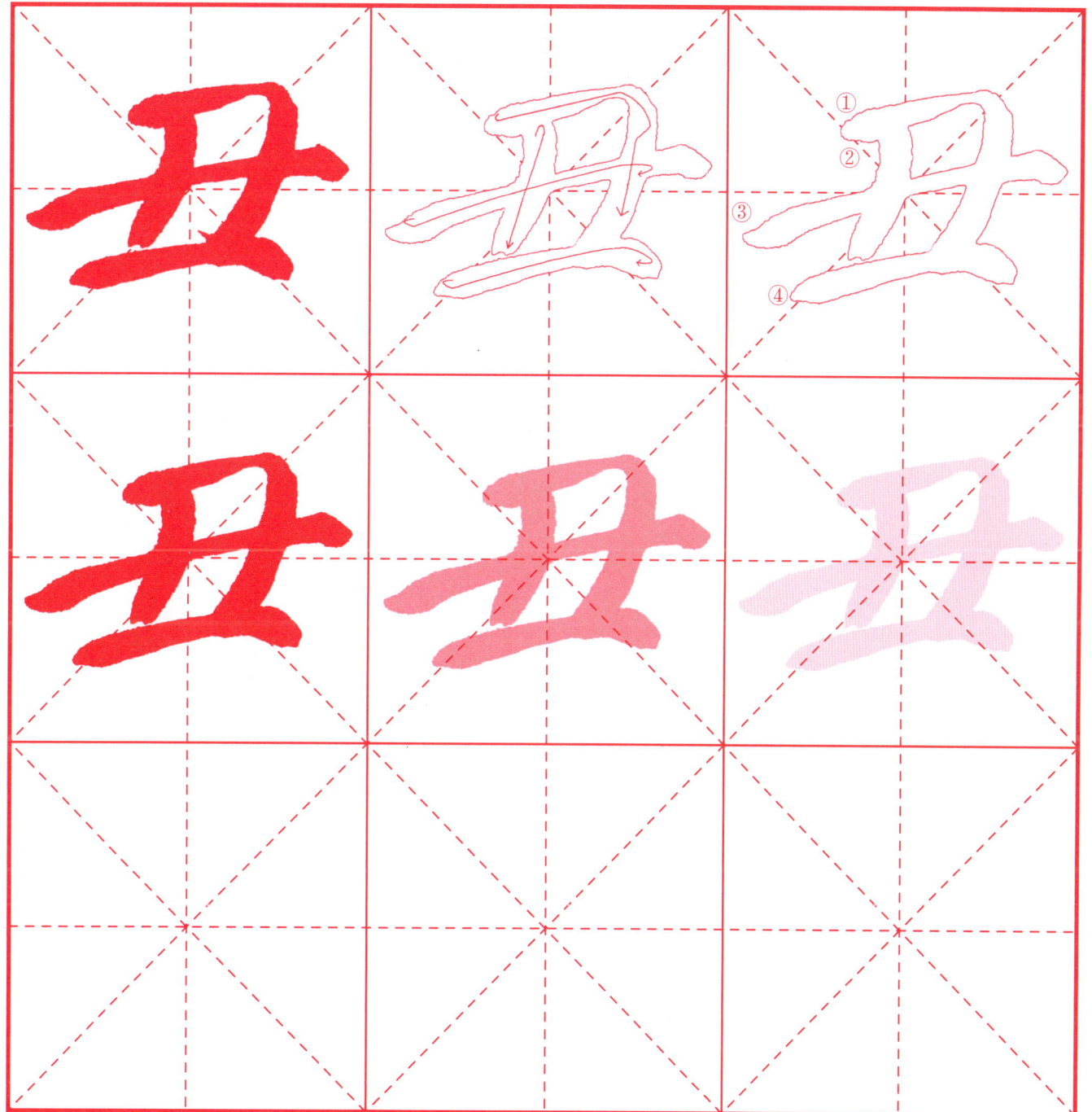

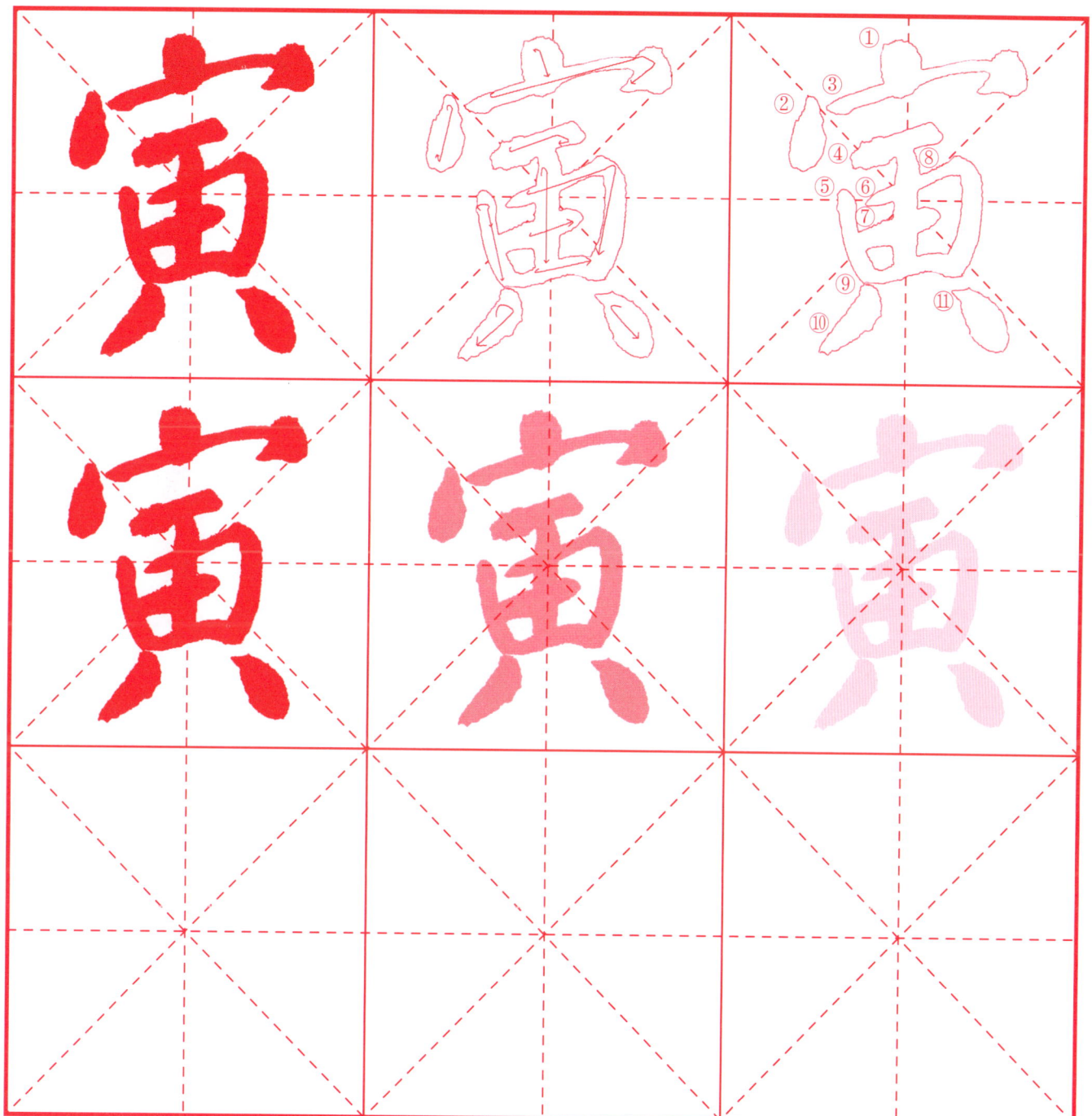

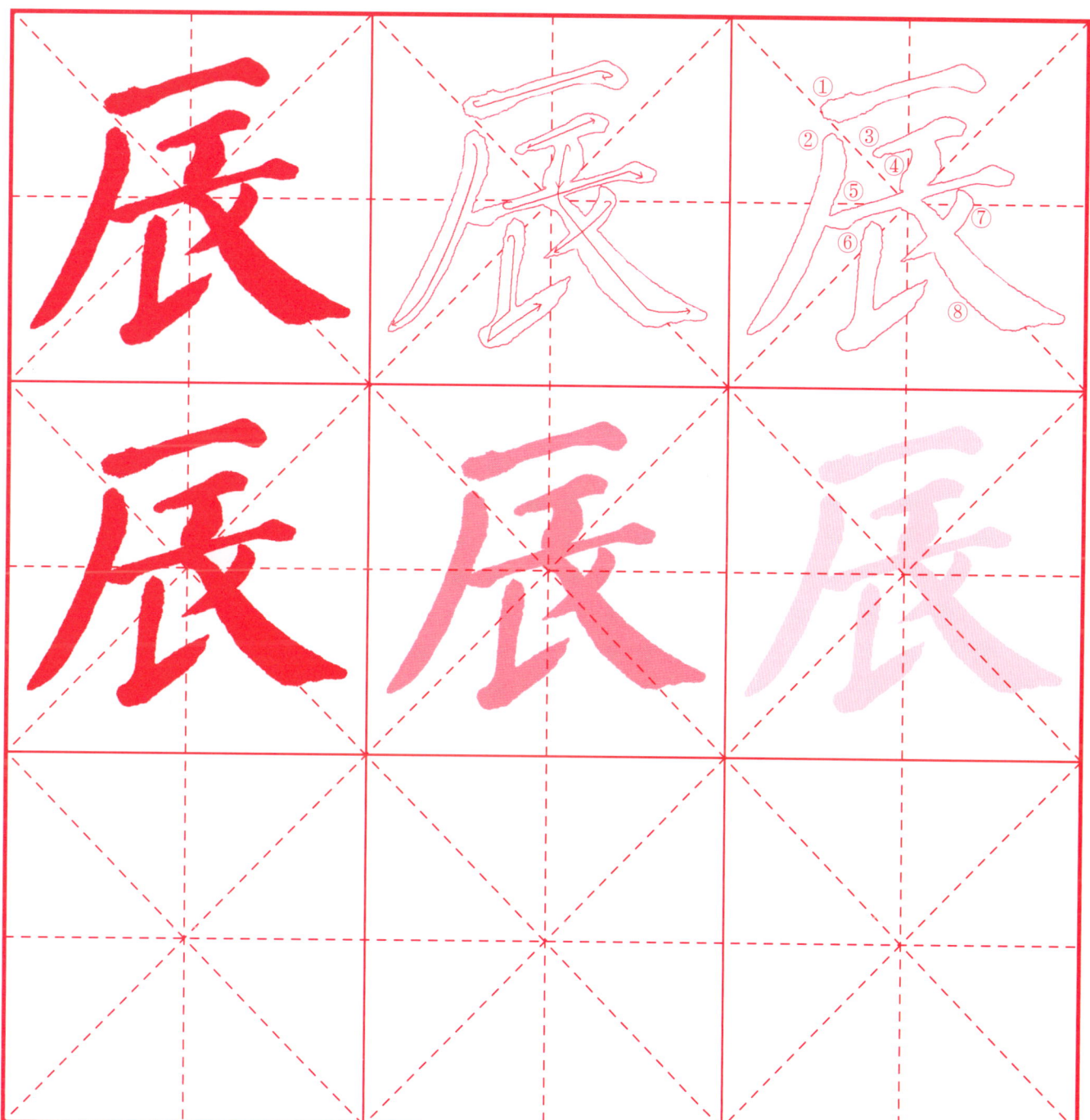

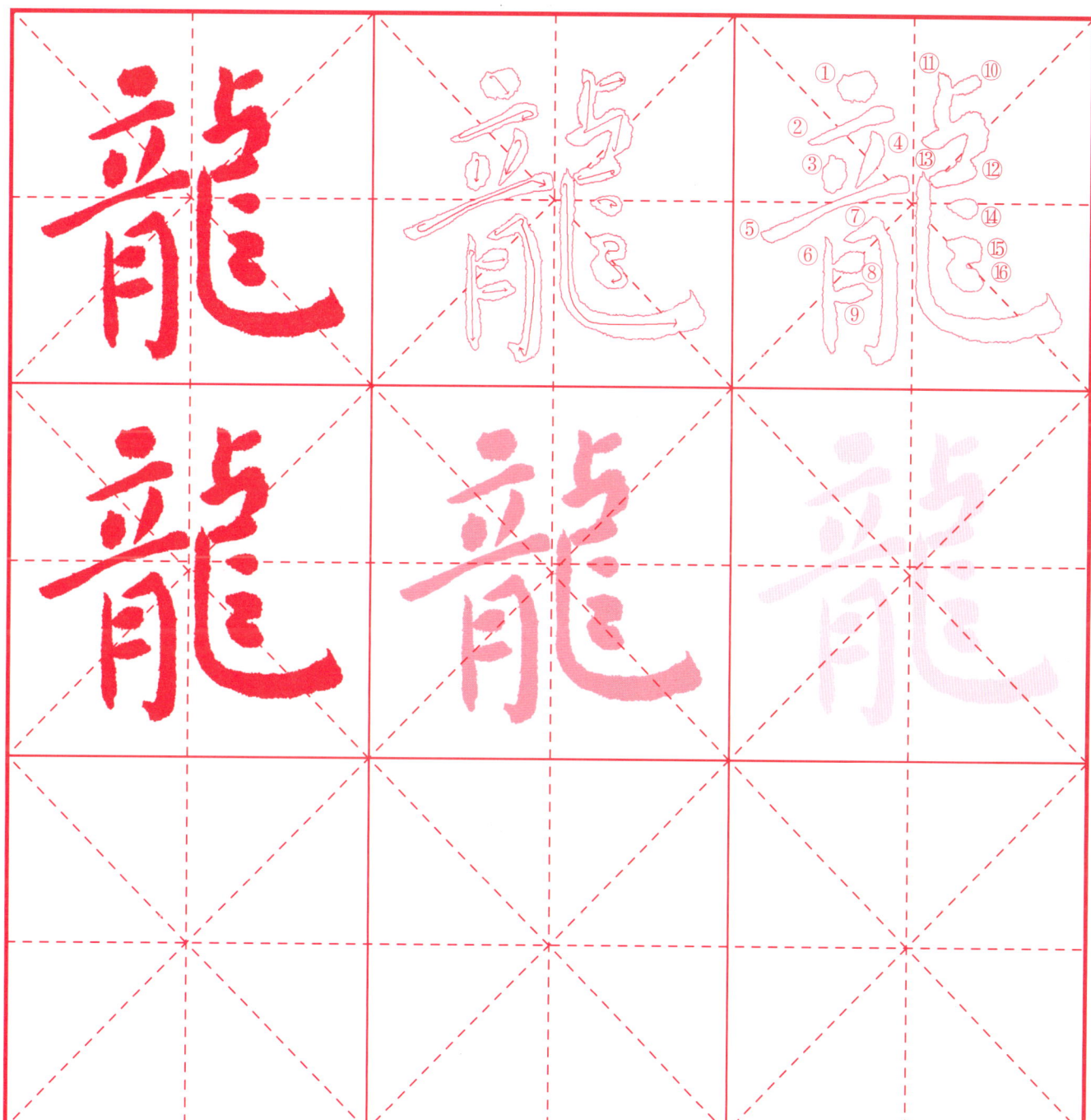

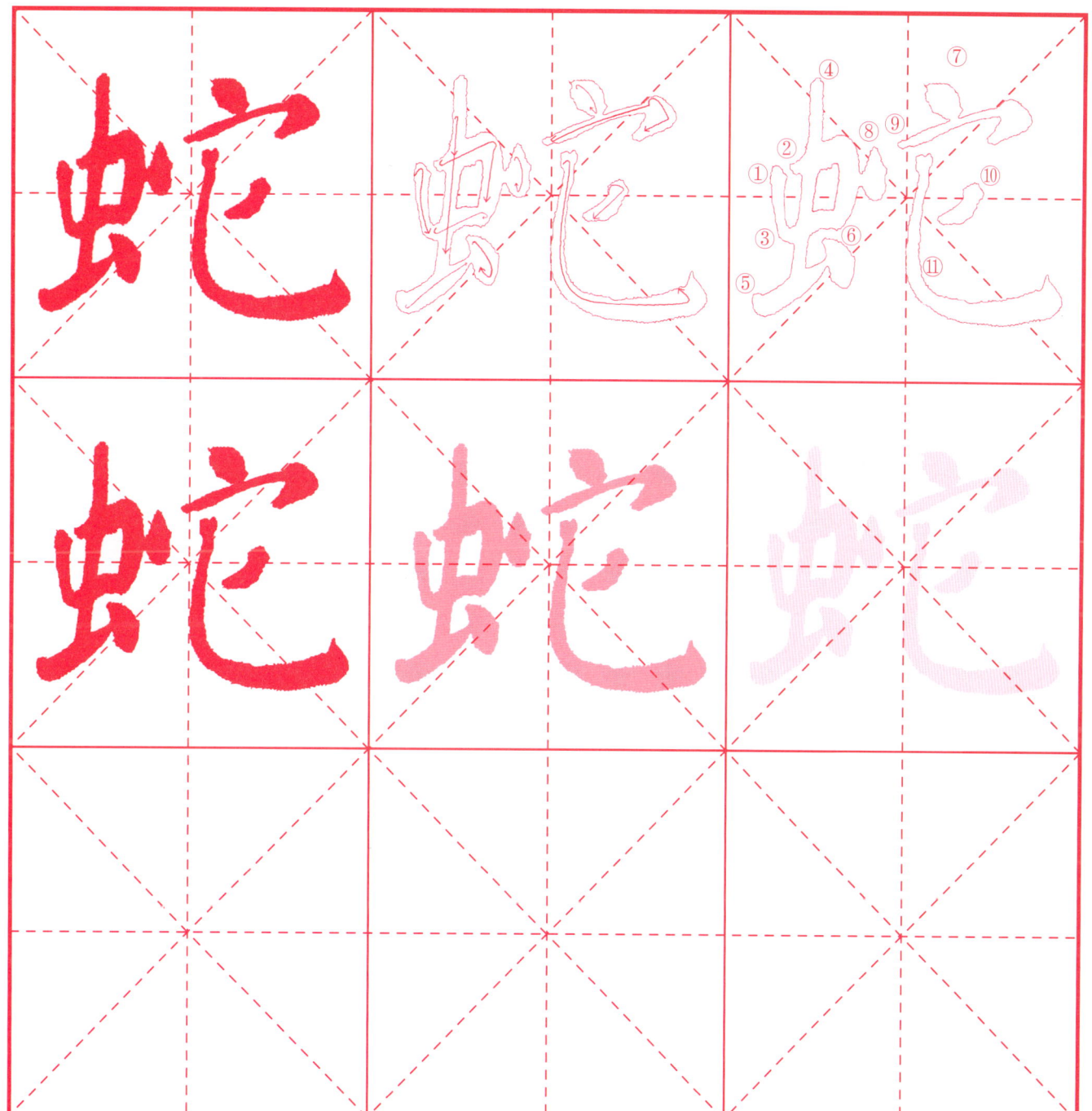

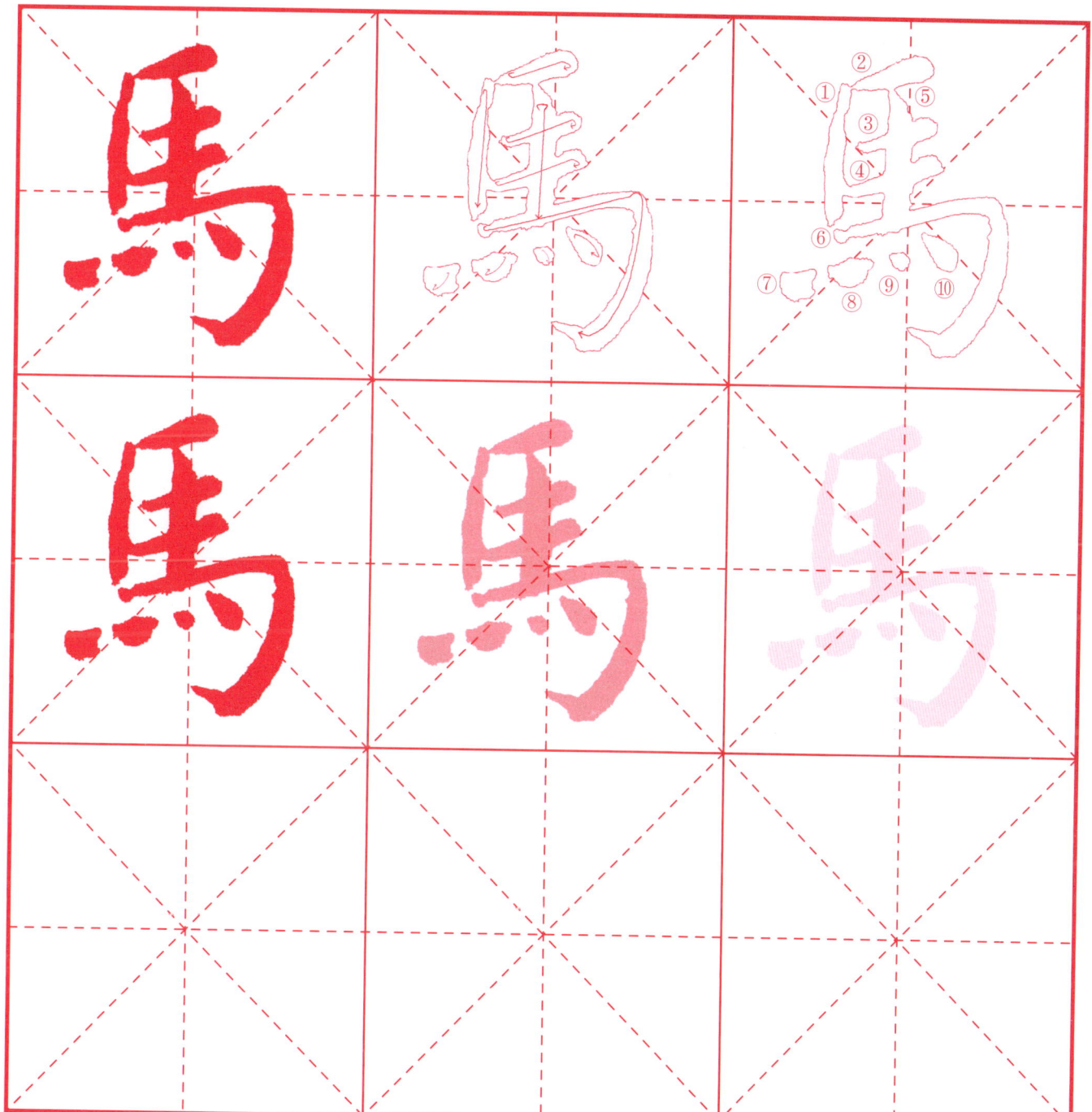

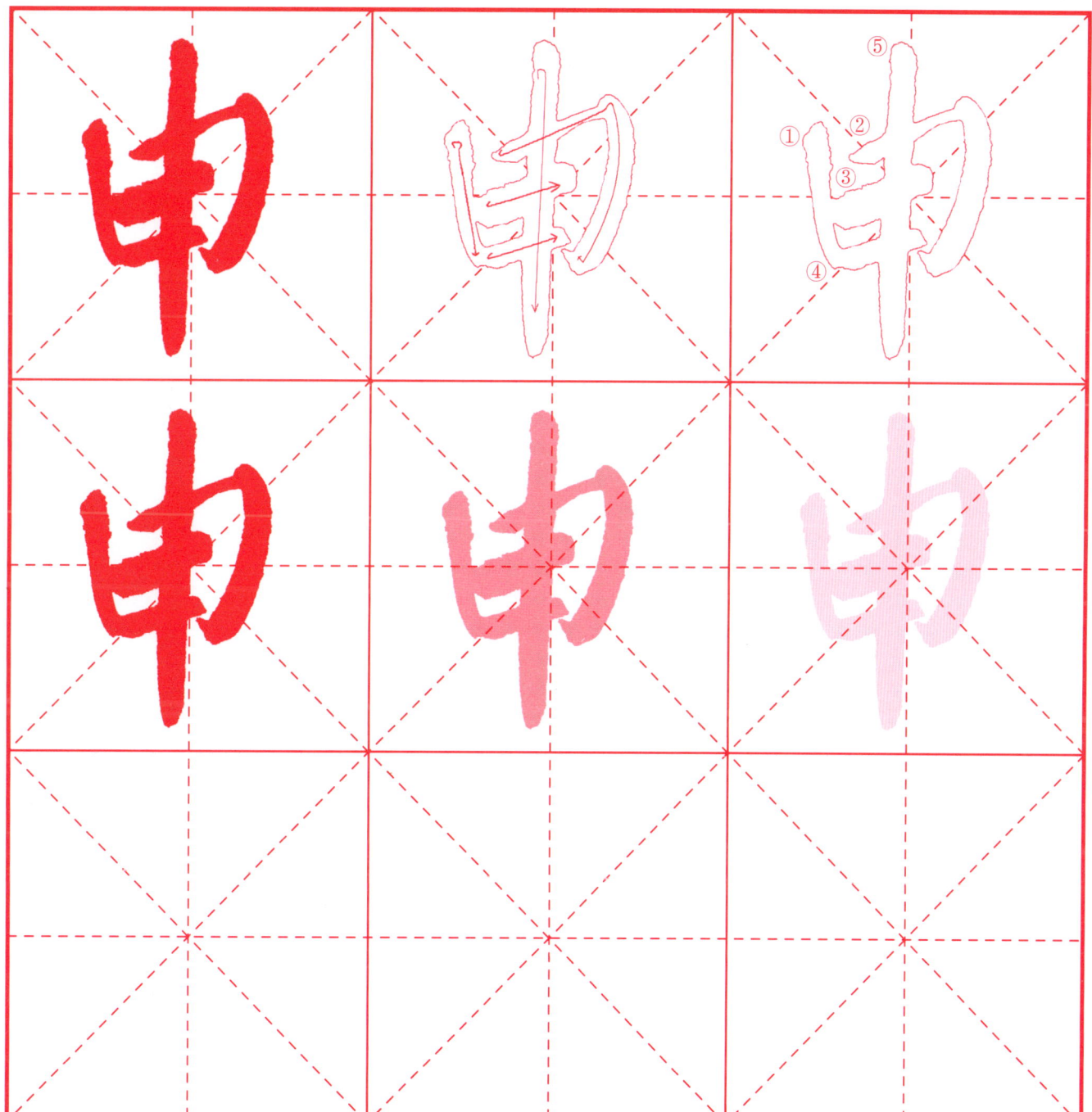

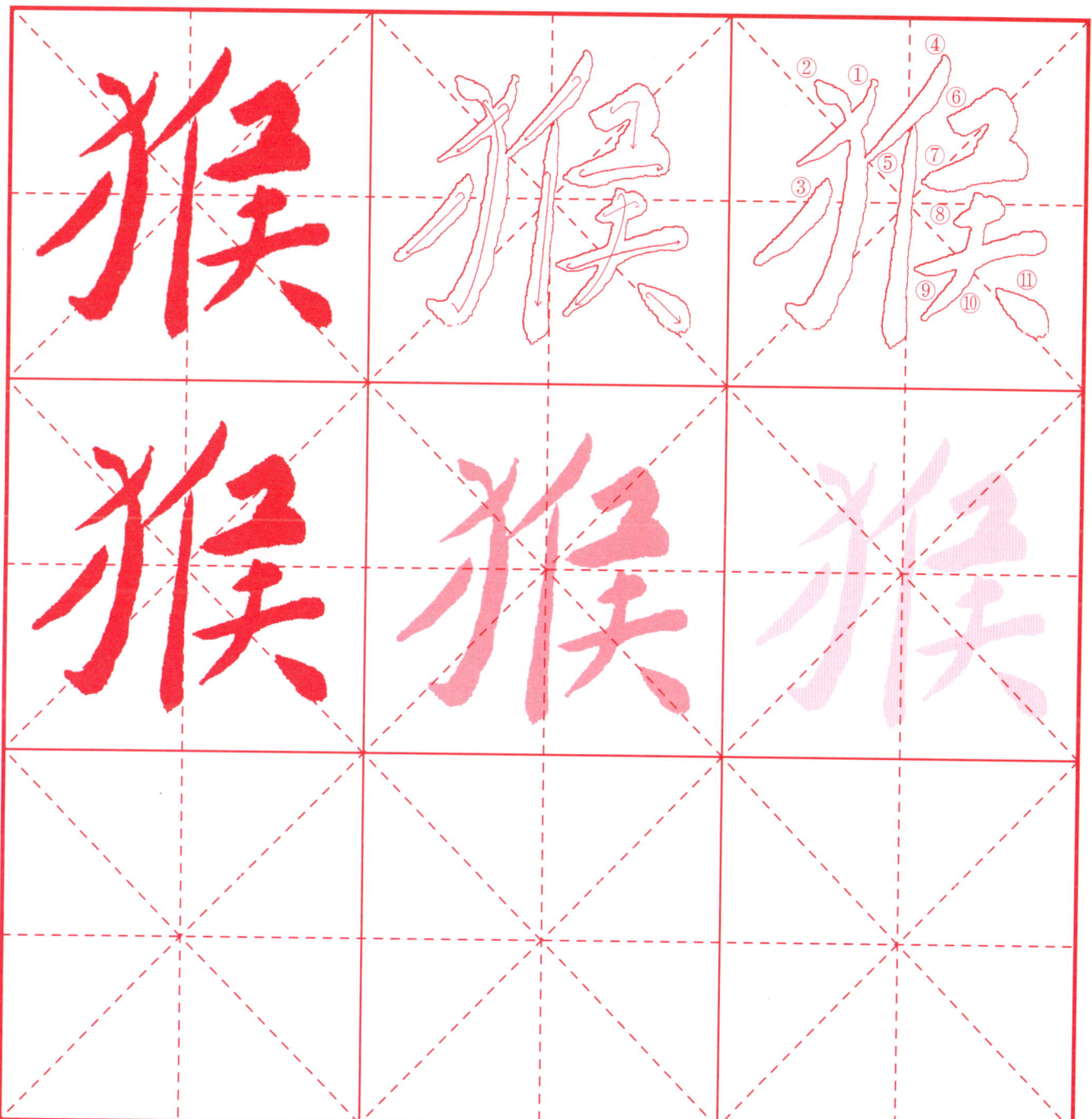

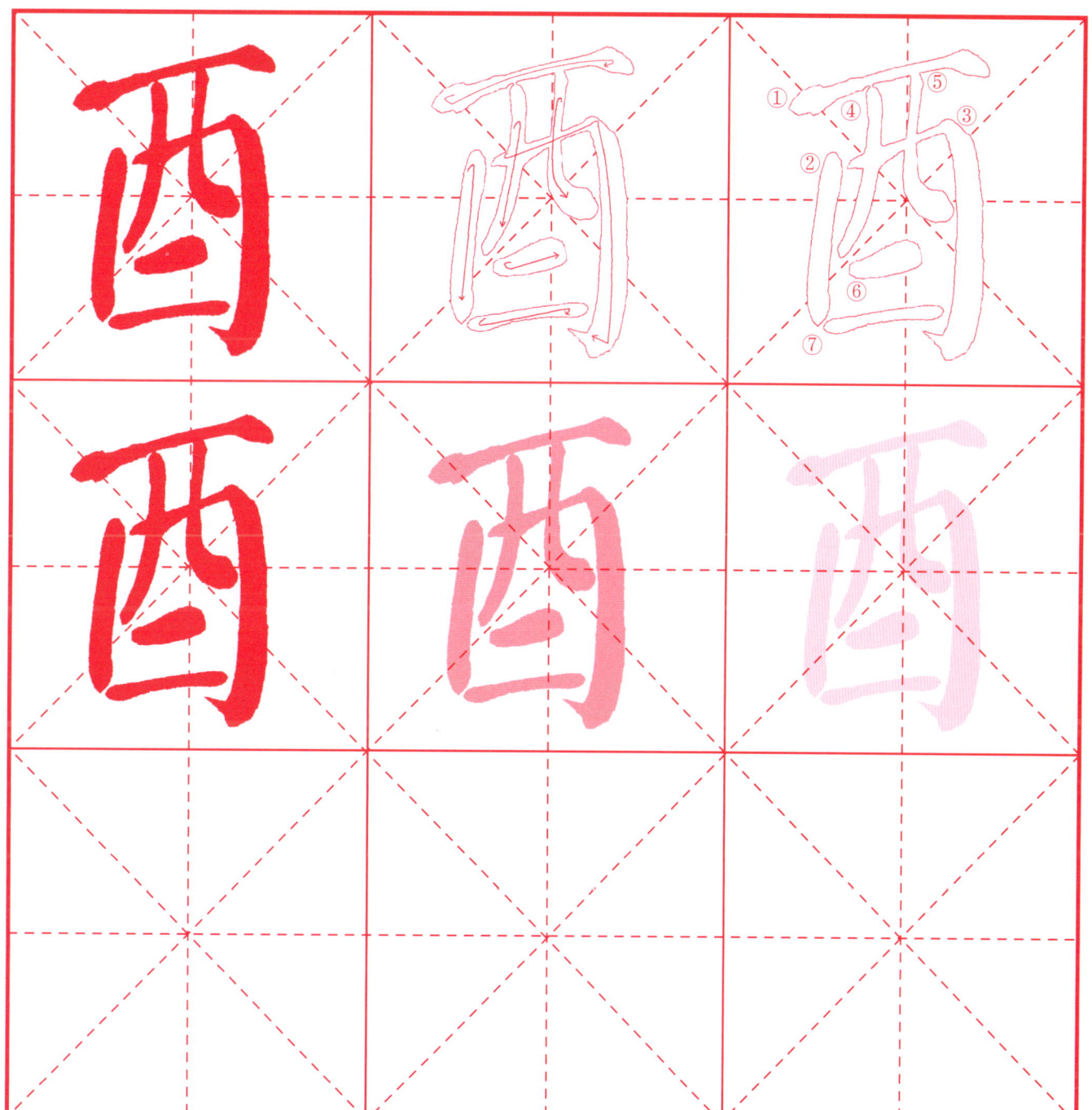

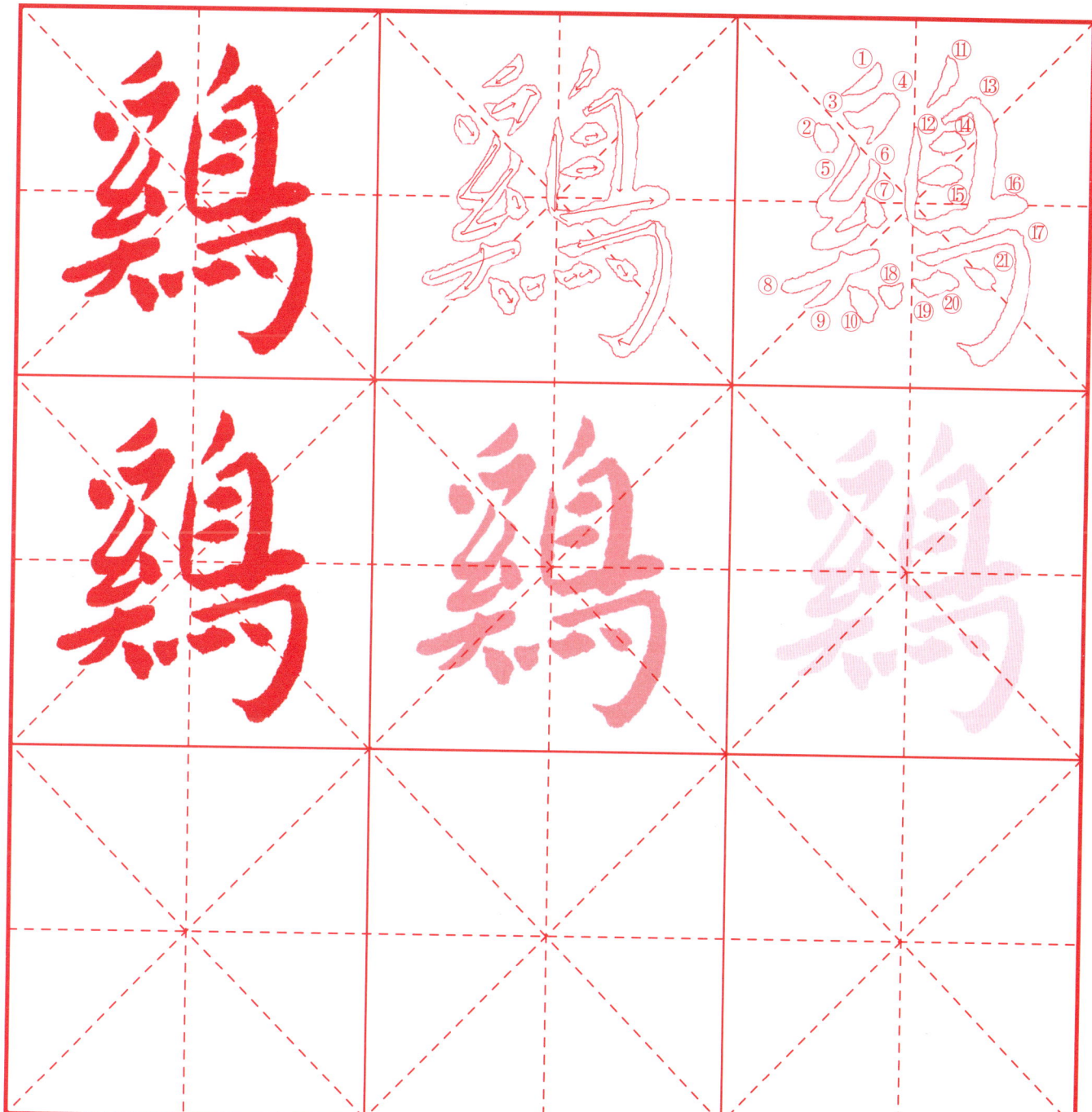

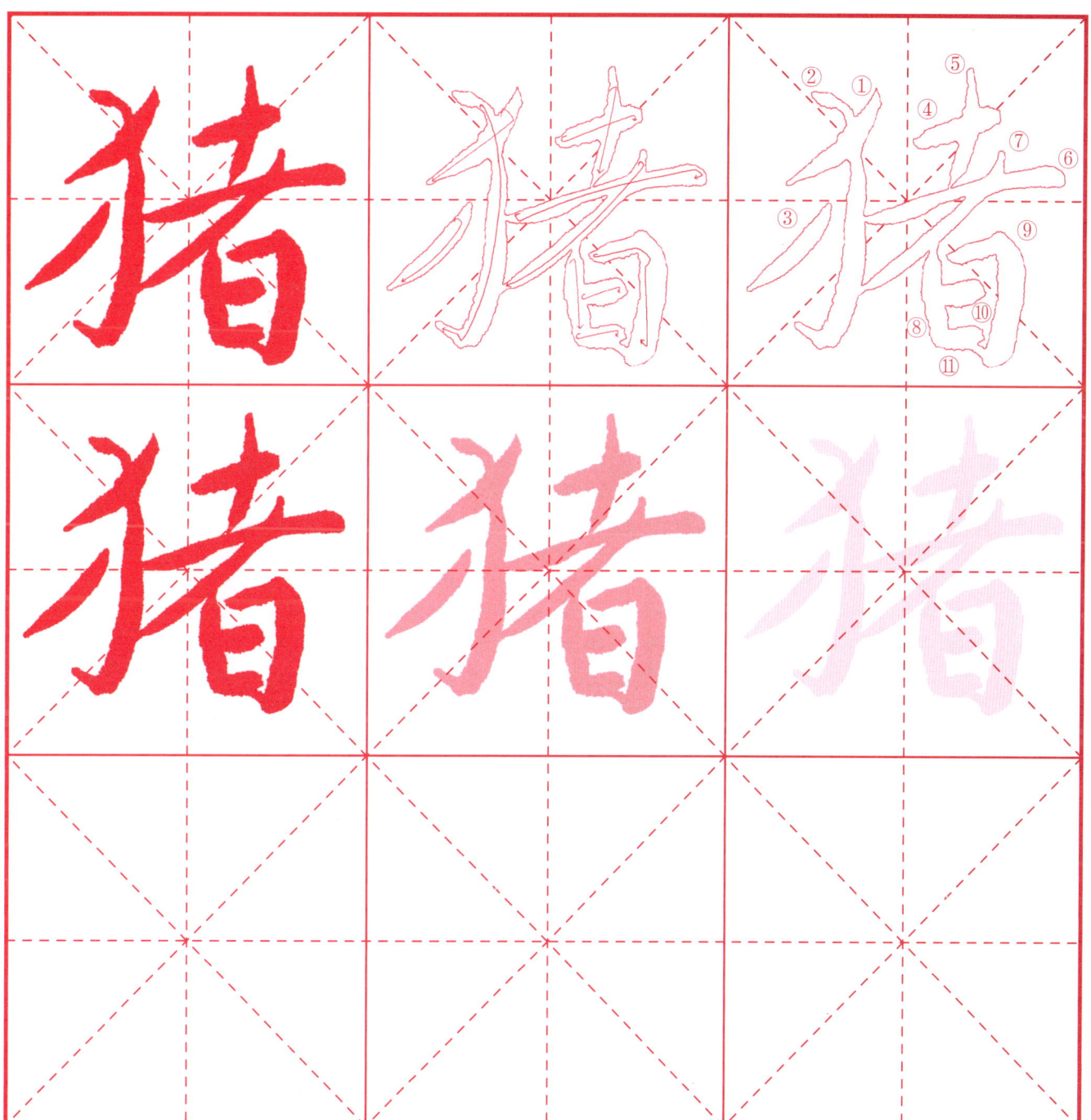